# LICENSE TO LIVE

# LICENSE TO LIVE

## A Manual for Getting Past Life's Roadblocks

ELVIN DOWLING

DESTINY IMAGE® PUBLISHERS, INC.

P.O. Box 310, Shippensburg, PA 17257-0310

*"Speaking to the Purposes of God for This Generation and for the Generations to Come."*

This book and all other Destiny Image, Revival Press, MercyPlace, Fresh Bread, Destiny Image Fiction, and Treasure House books are available at Christian bookstores and distributors worldwide.

For a U.S. bookstore nearest you, call **1-800-722-6774**.

For more information on foreign distributors, call **717-532-3040**.

Reach us on the Internet: **www.destinyimage.com.**

ISBN 13 TP: 978-0-7684-3695-2

ISBN 13 HC: 978-0-7684-3696-9

ISBN 13 LP: 978-0-7684-3697-6

ISBN 13 Ebook: 978-0-7684-9022-0

For Worldwide Distribution, Printed in the U.S.A.

1 2 3 4 5 6 / 14 13 12 11

# DEDICATION

To my family and friends for your continuing love and uncompromising support as I strived to complete this book—if it had not been for your willingness to support me in ways large and small, this work would not have seen the light of day.

To Cora Bannister Harper for never allowing me to give up on my dreams—because of you, this book was birthed.

To those I love who have gone on before me and those who have yet to come—thank you for your quiet inspiration.

To the youths who march onward and upward toward the light—never give up on your dreams.

# ENDORSEMENTS

*License to Live* is a must-read book for anyone striving to move past his or her mountains and turn obstacles into opportunities.

—Greg S. Reid
Speaker, Filmmaker, and Co-author, *Three Feet from Gold*

Elvin's life story is truly amazing and inspirational!

—Lia T. Gaines
President and Chief Executive Officer, CEO Ventures, Inc.

Elvin Dowling is the sort of man who is a facilitator. He gets things done. If there's a call to action, he's the man who hears that clarion call and steps up to the plate. Elvin Dowling is a true motivator.

—Wendell Pierce
Critically acclaimed and Award-Winning Actor
Played Detective William "Bunk" Moreland on HBO's "The Wire"

Each and every one of us wants more change in our lives— change meaning to make it bigger, better, brighter, more beautiful. And Elvin is the guy to do it because he is the leader of the Architects of Change.

—Mark Victor Hansen
Co-author, *Chicken Soup for the Soul*

Elvin Dowling's ability to overcome overwhelming obstacles—in spite of his circumstances—is a testament to the indomitable spirit inside each of us as we strive to live our dreams.

—Bill Stephney
Former President, Def Jam Recordings
Author, *Be a Father to Your Child*

I have witnessed Elvin's vitality, his ambition, and his passion for ministry. I am sure that young people and older people alike will be blessed by the Word of God as presented by this very powerful and anointed brother.

—Rev. Dr. Thomas D. Johnson Sr.
Senior Pastor, Canaan Baptist Church of Christ

Elvin obviously has a passion for the church and a calling that he is going to have the opportunity to fulfill.

—Ann Nobles
Senior Vice President, Eli Lilly Company

This book is going to touch thousands and thousands of people.

—John Mack
President, Los Angeles Police Commission

He's incredibly hardworking, diligent, and reliable. He has the highest integrity possible, but, more importantly, he's just a good guy!

—Tom Hyde
Executive Vice President, Wal-Mart Stores, Inc.

Elvin is an asset to any organization, any team. He is the go-to guy to solve problems. He has a generous spirit and a great sense of humor. I couldn't recommend him more highly.

—Melinda Emerson
The Small Biz Lady

# CONTENTS

# FOREWORD

*By Les Brown*

Every day as we are given an opportunity to live our lives with passion and fulfill our destinies with purpose, it is important to remember that we have a choice to make. We must choose each day to wake up out of a slumbering sleep and do something, or simply lay there and let life pass us by. Once we make that first and most important **decision**, however, everything else is left up to our own actions and the omnipotent will of a God who neither slumbers nor sleeps.

*"Must Jesus bear the cross alone, and all the world go free? No, there is a cross for every one...and there is a cross for me."*[1] Having grown up in humble beginnings on the floor of an abandoned building and given up for adoption by my birth mother, I can truly say that I have been blessed. My adoptive mother, Mrs. Mamie Brown, managed to instill in both myself and my twin brother Wesley a belief that I was better than no one else, but second to none as well. And that has made all the difference.

By all accounts, my life has been a great testament to the fact that, with hard work and determination, anything is possible. As a young student, I was labeled in educability as mentally retarded. But my mother, a single woman who had very little education herself, instilled within me a sense of hope and optimism that continues to buoy me to this day. With no formal education past high school, but with an unyielding determination, through the process of self-education I earned a master's degree in overcoming obstacles and my doctorate in human potential. Having started out as a local radio deejay, I served as a three-term state legislator, only to go on to make millions of dollars as a well-known professional speaker. Today, I know for myself that success is possible for those who refuse to accept the limits placed upon them by others. After all, there has never been a monument erected to honor a critic.

My friends, having experienced both the highs and lows of life, I know what it takes to succeed. I have had five PBS television specials, published books, and spoken to audiences of over 80,000 people around the world. I believe that you too can live your dream. You don't have to be great to get started, you just have to get started to be great! This book, *License to Live*, is an essential tool in helping each of us to plot our own "Real Life Road Map" to live our greatest life, with quality and satisfaction. It contains simple truths wrapped in a framework that most of us can understand—learning how to drive—and the universal rules that we can all learn from this common rite of passage as we travel along our way. Just as importantly, Elvin Dowling's compelling life story of triumph above tragedy continues to remind us throughout the pages of this book of just how blessed we really are.

Read this book. Take the test. Live with passion. Change the world!

# AUTHOR'S NOTE

As a means of disclaimer, I believe that it is important to note, from the beginning of this book, that I am a Christian. I believe that Jesus Christ is the Son of God and that He died to save me from my sins. Where I differ with many others in my faith, however, is that I also believe that Jesus Himself, by the very nature of who we as Christians believe He is, is a divisive figure—in terms of how those who believe otherwise see Him. Therefore I choose not to preach Jesus, but preach the gospel that Jesus preached: a hope-filled message of caring for the sick, advocating for the voiceless, and feeding the hungry in our society—all things men and women of goodwill can readily agree on. Who, after all, can argue with that? Moreover, I believe that as a Christian I am in no moral position to tell the Muslim, or the Jew, or the Hindu, or anyone else for that matter, that their religion is wrong and mine is right.

To that end, I encourage the believer and unbeliever alike to remember that there is but one God who keeps and sustains us all and to always remember that He sits up high and looks down low and loves us all equally. With that being said, I will refer to God, every now and again, when reflecting upon my life and where He has brought me from. I do so because He has been too good to me to not afford Him the credit He so richly deserves.

# STILL HERE

*"It doesn't matter where you start out in life; it's where you end up that counts."*

IT HAS often been said, "When life hands you a lemon, make lemonade!" Well, I am inclined to take it one step further and encourage you to open a lemonade stand! I was born the second child of an unwed, 18-year-old girl who had her first child at the tender age of 16. My father, by the time he had met my mother, had spawned so many other children out of wedlock that I was merely a notch in his bedpost and a fleeting nuisance—at best. So one could reasonably say that I came into the world with my own bag of lemons in tow!

But with those obstacles also came opportunities to make something of myself in spite of the odds, through sheer grit, determination, and the power of a helping hand. Considered by most who know me, however, to be a classic overachiever who refuses to become a statistic, I have a unique and storied background. My story started in an overcrowded apartment in a south Florida ghetto, wound its way through Capitol Hill in Washington, DC (and, from time to time, the White House), and landed on Wall Street in the financial capital of the world. I am blessed and highly favored. To say that God has been good to me is an understatement, however, when you consider the obstacles that were placed in my way and the losses that I have endured.

## My First Teachers

As a child growing up in a ghetto of West Palm Beach, Florida, my mother always taught me to appreciate life and the gift of the present and my father taught me, by the lack of his example no less, the power of forgiveness. For most of my childhood, my family eked out a meager and humble existence in the shadow of wealth and privilege. We were crammed into an overcrowded apartment off the mean streets of Pleasant City, the ironically named neighborhood from which I proudly hail, with its abysmal poverty, rampant crime, and continual hopelessness. Palm Beach County itself is a *Tale of Two Cities.* "It was the best of times, it was the worst of times...it was the age of wisdom...it was the season of Light."[1] On one side of the water you had the extraordinarily affluent island of Palm Beach, where I went to school with privileged children while my mother made their beds. She struggled just to keep a roof over our heads and depended upon food stamps and government assistance to help make ends meet. My mother taught me by the power of her example, however, that even though I was born in dire circumstances, dire circumstances weren't born in me!

My father, on the other hand, was an entirely different story. The example he set—a man chased by the living ghosts of abandoned children—was one that I chose not to follow as I became a father myself. I have sought to turn the pain of his absence as a stepping stone to my success, as I strive to walk in the newness of life.

When asked about the impact my mother had on me growing up as a child, I often remember the time that I learned how to cook. I was about 12 years old and called my mother from home, at her job, to tell her that I was hungry.

"Mama, I'm hungry," I cried as she listened somewhat impatiently on the other end of the phone.

"Well, did you cook you something to eat?"

"No."

"Well, you must not be that hungry!" Click.

She did that to me twice and I've been cooking ever since. My mother taught me self-determination. Our economic situation forced me to grow up and get over it. Those lessons have taught me to love my mama but to realize that she's not always going to be there. And long after she is gone, if I should succeed her, I'm going to have to take care of myself.

In 1972, famed Motown writers Norman Whitfield and Barrett Strong penned a hit song popularized by the group The Temptations that would go on to reach the top of the billboard charts and earn the group a Grammy award in 1973. The tune "Papa Was a Rollin' Stone" would come to symbolize the culture into which I was born in the fall of 1974. For me, it is a lyrical testimony to my fatherless childhood experience.

*"Papa was a rollin' stone,"* they sang, *"wherever he laid his hat was his home. And when he died, all he left us was alone."*

My biological father was a man who, I realized later on in my life, had simply gotten in over his head due to poor decision making and a lack of self-control when it came to fathering unwanted children who were virtually faceless to him. *"Hey mama...folks say papa was never much on thinkin',"* The Temptations crooned, *"Spent most of his time chasing women and drinkin'."*

What is unfortunate about my old man, however, is the fact that by walking away from his responsibility as father and friend he helped to perpetuate an epidemic. This epidemic would plague an entire generation of children, most of who looked just like me and came from similar circumstances.

*"Never got a chance to see him. Never heard anything but bad things about him. Mama I'm depending on you to tell me the truth..."*

My father was a recreational park director in my own neighborhood, prior to working at my high school full-time. He was a man who spent all of his time around children, yet he never had enough time for me. Later on in his life my father became a recognized community leader and church minister. Sadly, to my knowledge, he has never reconciled himself to the fact that there are children and grandchildren who bear his DNA whom he may never know. There are questions he has never answered and dreams he has never shared. In fact, in my father's case, he was more than just a rolling stone. He was an out-of-control snowball that ballooned into an avalanche of hurt and heartache for the children he left behind.

*"Heard some story about Papa in his storefront preachin'. Talkin' about savin' souls, and all the time leachin'. Dealin' in dirt! And stealing in the name of the Lord."*

Although the lack of his positive example was very difficult, I now realize that it was what made it possible for me to become the man I am today. I can now appreciate the indomitable spirit that his absence helped to create within me, and for that I will always be grateful.

Author Steven Ivory once observed:

Fatherhood is arguably the closest mortal man comes to Godliness. After all, according to the Good Book, God created man in his own image. Man, with profound assistance from a woman, more or less, does the same thing when his seed creates a child.[2]

As a father to a young boy, I endeavor to spend as much time as I can with my son, remembering what it felt like to have no father to spend time with me. As a result, I look forward to taking my son on outings and eating dinner with him every night, understanding that time is what is important and what he will remember long after I am gone.

Finally, my father has taught me, perhaps most importantly, that chains can be broken—and so can cycles. I am who he was not and, perhaps, may never be. I strive to do the exact opposite for my son of what he did for me. In doing so, I may not be a perfect father, but if I hit anywhere on the dartboard, I believe it will be an improvement.

Malcolm Gladwell, in his book *Outliers: the Story of Success*, poignantly underscores the importance of heritage and opportunity when it comes to those individuals who achieve some measure of success.

People don't rise from nothing. We do owe something to the parentage and patronage. The people who stand before kings may look like they did it all by themselves. But in fact, they are invariably the beneficiaries of hidden advantages and extraordinary opportunities and cultural legacies that allow them to learn and work hard and make sense of the world in ways others cannot.[3]

To that end, I want to declare my undying appreciation to both of my parents, the two greatest influences in my life, who taught me by the power of their example and the choices that they made. As my own man, however, I must walk my own path to become the person whom I was intended to be, and failure is not an option.

## Joy Comes in the Morning

When I was 6 years old, my favorite aunt was murdered by her boyfriend while her mentally impaired children looked on. On a hot summer's night in 1980, approximately one week before her 26th birthday, Clayether Dowling was brutally stabbed to death by her boyfriend, Robert, as my cousins Ricky and Tony watched in horror. Her sons, both severely mentally retarded, looked on in shock and confusion as he butchered my aunt with a kitchen knife, stabbing and slashing her more than a dozen times. All the while her next-door neighbors listened in and yet never bothered to call the police. Robert, a villainous and unrepentant gargoyle from the banks of Port-au-Prince, Haiti, harassed my aunt and stalked her for weeks before he finally fulfilled his deadly oath. "If I can't have you, no one will," he was heard to say as he snuffed out her brief life.

At my young age, I saw my auntie "Clay," my mother's older sister, as one of the most revered human beings I had come to know and love. Beautiful and stoic, graceful and divine, Clay was the epitome of a lady and a friend and didn't deserve to die in the manner in which she did. Though the circumstances surrounding her death were both heartless and horrific, I was later able to understand what the great political thinker, John Locke, meant when he declared that the nature of life was *"nasty, brutish and short."* Just live long enough! According to the Bureau of Justice Crime Statistics, in the year 2000, 33 percent of the female victims of homicide were killed by an intimate partner.[4]

I took two things away from this tragedy that continue to shape my life today: First, I must live each day as if it were my last and plan each day as if I will live forever. Second, if someone threatens to kill you—believe them! "More truth is told inside a joke than truth is told alone." Now, imagine the truth spoken in anger!

When I was 14, my first cousin, James Denard Dowling, nick-named "Nard" for short, was kidnapped, murdered, and dumped along the side of the road because of the poor decisions that he had made. Like most people who make poor decisions that lead them to untimely fates, Nard was a good person who did stupid stuff—like hanging around with the "dope boys" of Palm Beach County. An 18-year-old computer science student with dreams of one day marrying and moving away, the violence of the streets caught up with him for a third and fatal time in the summer of 1990. His death, chronicled in the local newspaper, *The Palm Beach Post*, was both horrific and sad, "His body was found Tuesday alongside Beeline highway about a mile south of PGA Blvd. There were nine bullets in his stomach, police said."[5] The life of a promising young man had been snuffed out senselessly because he picked the wrong "homeys." ("With friends like that who needs enemies?")

Studies show that:

Homicide is estimated to account for fourteen percent (14%) of the life expectancy difference between black and white men, occurring predominantly in the younger ages. Even when socio-demographic factors such as age, employment status, income, education and marital status held constant, black men are over five times more likely to be victims of homicide than white men.[6]

The very next year, James' brother McGill was murdered as he stood on a street corner in the neighborhood we grew up in and called our own. Several years after that we lost their sister LaShaun, who succumbed to the AIDs virus, leaving behind two small children and those who loved her most.

At 19 years old, I buried my brother Bryant. Bryant Carltise Proby, my half-brother with whom I share a mother, was a brand-new dad struggling to turn his life around when he was gunned down. He was shot in the head while he sat in his newly remodeled convertible Chevy Impala, staining the interior with the color of blood that turns a burgundy-brown when it spills from the body. This occurred in broad daylight just one block away from the church that we both grew up in, on a corner filled with people—and nary a witness to be found. There lay my brother, dead at 21 years old.

In his touching article, "A Black Man Dies: Why Is It Only His Mother Cries?" journalist William Cooper recounted the losses endured by a growing, silent minority.

You didn't know Steven Henry McClendon, but you know his profile. Young black male dead at nineteen. Gunshot wound to the head. Sunday afternoon, another young African-American, Bryant Proby, 21, was fatally shot in the head while he sat in his convertible on Fourth Street near Tamarind Avenue. Proby was homicide 78.[7]

The loss of Bryant was wounding to me in a way that was debilitating at the worst of times and revelatory at others. In his poem, "Invictus," William Ernest Henley thanked "whatever gods may be" for his unconquerable soul. "In the fell clutch of circumstance," he declared, "my head is bloody but unbowed."[8] To some, this loss was a mere footnote in the evening paper, an inevitable statistic, but to me it was personal. "You see, a statistic means nothing until it affects you or those you love...In fact, the hard odds against our success can seem cruel and insurmountable unless we are exposed to those who buck the odds."[9]

To add heartache to pain, a year later, Rodriguez Dante Barfield, my half-brother with whom I share a father, was killed. He had just hit the rap scene as an up-and-coming hip-hop artist with dreams of superstardom. Dante, a brother who always spoke his mind, which sometimes got him into trouble, was killed by a so-called friend over a petty argument about nothing. Because of the recent notoriety of Dante, known by his rap name as Nena, and his group, the local paper followed the story of his death and the subsequent arrest of his murderer.

A local rap singer who burst onto the national music scene last month with a song about killing on the streets was gunned down blocks from his home early Wednesday.... He just signed a record deal. Now he's dead.[10]

Many people do not realize that Palm Beach County, Florida, is extraordinarily violent. Economically, politically, and culturally, it is an oppressive place to live for minorities and individuals of color. Moreover, the pain we feel as minorities is oftentimes internalized into an abysmal self-loathing that allows the oppressed to continue wearing their chains of bondage long after the "master" has left the scene.

Oppression is the systematic, institutionalized mistreatment of one group by people of another group for whatever reason….The flip-side of oppression is internalized oppression. Members of the target group are emotionally, physically, and spiritually battered to the point that they begin to believe that their oppression is deserved, is their lot in life, is natural and right and that doesn't even exist. The oppression begins to feel comfortable, familiar enough that when 'mean ol' Massa lay down the whip, we got's to pick up the whip and whack ourselves and each other.[11]

## The Last Man Standing

I have been through too many traffic accidents to count, almost drowned in the middle of the ocean, and had my house shot up while I slept inside. Yet through it all, I'm still here and that, I believe, is for a reason. Today, I am living proof that even when mountains are placed in your way, all things are possible if you only just believe and never **ever** give up. My story is quintessentially American and will resonate within the hearts and minds of those who root for the underdog. In fact, I would venture to say that in many ways, you and I are just alike. I suspect that you may be reading this book because you are convinced that there has to be something better in this life for you and you're searching for an answer. If you believe that the sky is the limit, and the limit should not be the sky, then this book is for you. If you are ready to embrace change and achieve greatness, hold on to your seats. If, as Fannie Lou Hamer once declared, you are "sick and tired of being sick and tired" of life passing you by, I hope you'll come along for the ride. ("No one can save us, for us, but us. If it is to be...it's up to me!")

Poet David Herbert Lawrence once wrote, "I never saw a wild thing sorry for itself. A small bird will drop frozen dead from a bough without ever having felt sorry for itself."[12] As an individual who could very well use the excuse of my undesirable upbringing to do the wrong things and become a drain on society, being from a "broken home" and all, I've had a-million-and-one reasons to quit. When I feel like throwing myself a pity party, however, I am quickly reminded of the fact that someone else always has it worse off than me. ("I used to complain about having no shoes until I saw a man who had no feet.") In his bestselling book, *Reposition Yourself*, Bishop T.D. Jakes reminds us that everyone has challenges to face in life, but the true test of character lies in how we respond when called to rise to the occasion. Jakes observed:

Life is not fair. You will have to overcome odds that may be stacked against you. But you can change the outcome of your life if you will refuse to give up hope and each day refine your vision of who you really are. It will require a new way of thinking.[13]

## How to Use This Book

*License to Live: A Manual for Getting Past Life's Roadblocks* is here to inspire you to overcome your own odds. It is a fusion of Jack Canfield and Mark Victor Hansen's *Chicken Soup for the Soul* with Joseph Conrad's classic *Heart of Darkness*. Or, in the lyrics of Frankie Beverly and Maze, a little bit of "Joy and Pain." It is a unique blend of tragedy and triumph, served up with a homespun helping of hope and inspiration from a

Generation Next perspective. Moreover, this book is not just about showing you how, through very simple steps, you can truly live your best life, it is also a permit to free yourself from the shackles of pain and death that continue to hold you back. Whether you've experienced a death in your finances, a death in your family, or a death in your relationships, this book will help you to overcome these obstacles and roadblocks to your dreams.

I have heard it said, "Wisdom is learning from the mistakes of others and experience is learning from your own mistakes." My life's experiences and the lessons that grew from them are the basis by which I offer you a simple formula for living the life you have always wanted. So that most people who read this book have a frame of reference upon which to draw as they navigate this new road map to their own success, I have expanded upon an application that speaks to almost everyone: learning how to drive and earning a license. Driving, after all, is something that we can almost do with our eyes closed. (I did say *almost*.) Moreover, while reading this book, you will relearn the steps it takes to become an excellent driver on the streets of success as you travel along your way.

Throughout this book, I will frame the harsh realities of my upbringing as *Red Light Challenges* and will show you how to avoid them. How I reacted to those challenges I call my *Roadside Responses*, and they will help you to MapQuest a detour around the mistakes that I have made so that you don't create potholes of your own. I take a stroll down memory lane in what I call my *Rearview Glances* and share with you stories and anecdotes to fill your tank along the way. The life lessons learned become *Universal Road Rules* that will serve as directional signs along the highways of life as you ease on down the road. Finally, I will provide you with a series of action steps that will serve as your very own *Real Life Road Map:* directions, suggestions, and tips to help you take action now as you strive to fulfill your destiny.

Finally, my friend, as you turn the pages of this book and write a new chapter for your life, I have one request to ask of you: please read through to the end. The answers you've been looking for may be just a paragraph away. After all, "Objects in mirror are closer than they appear." Get your motor running. Head out on the highway. You have greatness within you!

PART
ONE

Chapter I

# HAVING A LICENSE IS A PRIVILEGE

EACH YEAR since 1976, the National Urban League issues what it calls the *State of Black America* report. The 2007 report contains startling data about the status of black males that ought to make us all cringe, including the fact that they disproportionately make up a majority of America's prison population and live shorter, sicker, and more broken lives than most people within our society.

> Black men have higher mortality rates than white men at every age. It is only among adults older than age sixty-five, where this disparity begins to decline. This "survivor effect" demonstrates that if one can survive to old age, the mortality rate is roughly equal.[1]

As an African-American male myself, I know that these statistics are real because I have survived to tell the tale.

> It [being a young, black male in American society today] means to be a member of a group who is the disproportionate victim of homicide. It means to be a member of a group whose rate of suicide is increasing astronomically in comparison to other

populations. It means to be a member of a group whose labor force status is declining enormously, as evidenced by high rates of joblessness.[2]

In Langston Hughes' rhyme, *Mother to Son*, the poet wrote: *"Life for me ain't been no crystal stair. It's had tacks in it, and splinters, and boards torn up, and places with no carpet on the floor—bare."*[3] Having been born a black male in America at the height of the Watergate scandal, I entered American society at the bottom of the social ladder. Today, however, in the age of Obama, where a black man has risen to the rank of president of the United States of America, society no longer accepts the "poor black guy excuse." My mentor and teacher, Eric B. Bailey, often reminded me of that fact long before Barack Obama entered the national political scene.

"But Mr. Bailey, they won't let me because I don't have the money," I would say. "I can't because I'm black."

"Elvin, cut the crap," he would reply. "That's life! What's life? A magazine. Where do you buy it? A newsstand. How much? Five cents. Don't have it? That's tough. What's tough? Life. What's life? A magazine..."

You see, it keeps going and going, just live long enough. In a 21st-century world, particularly in America, with the right opportunities, strategic assistance, and personal will, anything is possible. Life itself is a right and every day is a gift, which is why they call it "the present." To live your one life to the fullest, however, is a privilege that few get to enjoy. But as long as you're breathing, there's hope and it's possible.

Each day billions of people around the world wake up and, almost as if on autopilot, exercise the privilege they have earned from a recognized licensing bureau to operate a motor vehicle on the streets, roads, and highways of the places they live and love. What each of these individuals can attest to (or at least most of them will) is the fact that they had to complete a process of study and testing. After they passed, they were afforded the privilege of driving and given a license to operate a motor vehicle. Moreover, to forget that this license does not actually belong to the driver but to the entity that issued it is a one-way street to having those same privileges revoked. In New York State, for example, an individual's license can be suspended or cancelled by the Department of Motor Vehicles:

> "Suspension is when your license, permit or privilege is taken away for a period of time before it's returned. Revocation is when your license or permit or privilege to drive is cancelled."[4]

Reasons for suspension or elimination of one's driving privileges in New York State, and around the world, include DWI (Driving While Intoxicated), homicide, assault, criminal negligence resulting in death from the operation of a motorized vehicle, leaving the scene of an accident, no insurance, and failure to answer a ticket or pay a fine.

So, to proceed with some semblance of clarity, I will define the terms "right" and "privilege" using the legal terminology outlined in *The Gilbert Law Dictionary*. As such, a *right* is defined as:

> Inherent power or privilege to freely act; an inherent privilege or interest which is recognized by the power of law (i.e. in the United States, the "Bill of Rights" which guarantees the right to worship freely and the right against self incrimination, etc.).[5]

Conversely, a *privilege* is defined as:

Some advantage or benefit enjoyed by one person or a particular group of persons; a benefit which all citizens do not share; a specific immunity (i.e. physician-patient privilege).[6]

Failure to understand the difference between rights and privileges can lead to significant and material discomfort.

## You Were Born to Drive

Perhaps the greatest responsibility that every driver bears is the fact that having a license is a privilege that can be revoked at any time, for any reason. As a new driver starting out, this is the first thing we are taught: driving has the power to deliver or destroy with one press of the pedal. When trying to navigate the highways of life, which are filled with twists and turns, it is important that we remember this. Even though we were each born with a God-given right to be free, driving is a benefit that we enjoy only through the licensing process. In the Preamble to the Constitution of the United States, Thomas Jefferson declared:

We hold these truths to be self evident that all men are created equal and are endowed by their Creator with certain inalienable rights, that among these are life, liberty and the pursuit of happiness.

Within this well-worn credo lies a certain fundamental principle that governs all of God's children, regardless of their station or lot in life: we are each given specific and implied rights inherent in us at birth.

As members of the human race, we were all born to drive down the highways of life. Moreover, lying deep within each of us is an innate desire to get our motors running. But whether we get in the driver's seat and take life for a spin is up to each and every one of us.

In the United Nations-backed International Bill of Human Rights, inalienable rights are more broadly described:

All human beings are born free and equal in dignity and rights. They are endowed with reasonable conscience and should act towards one another in a spirit of brotherhood.[7]

As members of the global family, it is incumbent upon each of us to understand that we are, indeed, born with the capacity to live a life beyond our wildest imaginations, all of which is buttressed by basic rights which cannot be abridged. Even if you are like me and started out in the race of life with a ball and chain fastened to your legs, the race to the top isn't over until you win. Having grown up in less-than-favorable conditions, all I knew was struggle. Today, however, having overcome many challenges that confound the imagination, I stand solidly convinced that if I can make it, so can you. You are somebody—have been from birth—because "God don't make no junk!"

 **Red Light Challenge:
"Mama's Baby. Papa's Maybe?"**

My friends from school always lived better than me, with regard to material things—and had the trust funds to prove it. In fact I often joke that we were so poor, as a child I would wear holes on the soles of my shoes so big that "I could step on a quarter and tell you if it was heads or tails." One time in particular, I went to my father, who had abandoned me as a baby but whom I saw every day as a teenager because he worked at my high school as a custodian, and asked him to buy me a new pair of shoes. Now mind you, I was already conditioned by my mother to not expect anything from my father, let alone some new kicks to start off the school year. Nonetheless, the need was urgent. My "dogs were truly barking" so I approached him anyway. (For those who aren't from the 'hood, that simply means that the soles had separated from the shoes and appeared to be talking when you walked. Now, back to business.)

I will never forget asking my father for money to help me get a new pair of shoes, to which he responded: "I have rent to pay." He then abruptly walked away. This was the second and final time that I would allow him to disappoint me in such a manner. At 8 years old, I had stood outside his apartment on the balcony, as he wouldn't let me in to meet his new wife and other children, and pleaded with him to buy me a new bicycle for Christmas that year. Of course, he promised that he would and promptly reneged on his commitment. Christmas came and Christmas went and nary a bike to be found. Even still, in spite of his complete abdication of his role as my father and my friend, I am crazy enough to believe God when He assures me, *"When my father and my mother forsake me, then the Lord will take me up"* (Ps. 27:10).

Later on in life, I would have the opportunity to invite my father to my wedding, which I did more for me than for him. He didn't make it, but at least I did my part. No matter, my most important day was celebrated by family and friends (including two members of Congress, a former big city mayor, and two presidents of national organizations) and the people who truly loved me. A ten-piece band also helped us to kick the festivities off rather nicely. I did hear from him eventually, when he saw me in the April 2005 issue of *Ebony Magazine*[8] as one of the "Thirty Leaders of the Future." Even after all the time we have missed together, it was still nice to get my father's approval. That means a lot, when you think about it.

Unfortunately, for large swaths of the American family, many dining room chairs remain empty every night. In droves, men have abandoned their most sacred responsibility as role models for their own families first and then for the community. As a member of the black community, it goes without saying, unfortunately, that this phenomenon has become all too commonplace for those of us who missed a father's influence on our daily lives.

For many African-American families and communities, father disengagement and marginalization has become not a cultural shame but a cultural norm. According to a recent Child Trends Data bank report, 69.5% of African-American children are born to unmarried mothers in comparison to 47.9% of Hispanic children, 25.4% of white children and 16.2% of Asian/Pacific Island children.[9]

Even still, many a talented individual has risen above these abysmal statistics to take the world by storm and break the chains of hopelessness that have become a way of life for far too many. As a victim of neglect by my own father, I understand the debilitating effects that parental absence can have in one's life and how easily our parent's failures can, if we are not careful, come to define our future.

### Roadside Response: "Acknowledge the Past, Reclaim the Future"

As a result of what I learned from my own father, I now look forward with joyful anticipation to taking my son on outings and eating dinner with him every night. I understand that the time I spend with him is what is most important and what he will remember long after I am gone. Every evening, for example, I make a point of rushing home from wherever I may be to eat dinner with my family. My wife and I spend quality time together, play games, and adhere to a consistent bedtime ritual that includes reading, singing, and loving our children "to pieces." Most recently, I took my son to Sesame Place theme park in Pennsylvania where I, myself, acted like a 2–year-old. I splashed along on the water rides and other fun attractions with my giggling little boy who seemed to have the time of his life. We took photos with Elmo and did all the things that I always wanted to do when I was a child myself. Some may say that, in more ways than one, I am reliving the missing components of my childhood vicariously through my own son, and perhaps they would be correct. Through this bonding time, however, I have discovered that the best things in life are truly free.

I am more than compensated for my efforts by the smile of a little boy who lights up like a Christmas tree at the very mention of "Daddy" or at the moment I walk into a room. Moreover, in the still of the night, when I am awakened by the cries of a scared young boy who can only be soothed by "Daddy," I am reminded of why the calling to fatherhood is one that should not be entered into lightly or unadvisedly. Just as importantly, I am enormously grateful for the gift of my child who, through the very nature of his presence in my life, has helped to change me in ways large and small, helping me to focus on the things that are important. The point, my friend, is simple: If I don't teach my own son how to be a man and the importance of standing on his own two feet, nobody else is going to do it.

To some extent, as an almost overzealous parent, I am a victim of my own success. For example, when I do have to leave the house for a business trip or an extended absence of a day or more, my son often cries as if there is no tomorrow. He just simply does not want "Daddy" to leave him. What he does not realize, however, is that every tear he sheds for me to never leave him makes it all the more urgent that I hurry home real soon because he needs me. More importantly, in the eyes of someone else, I am their world. And though my previous experiences were colored by the fact that my father was not there, I choose not to repeat that cycle with my son.

Having often been the only father in the pediatrician's waiting room or at Thursday morning Gymboree classes, I take my role as being "that dad" very seriously. When I served as chief of staff of one of the largest social advocacy networks in the world, many co-workers were sometimes befuddled at my insistence upon leaving work early enough to tuck my child in at night. Whatever was going on at the moment the clock struck 5:00 P.M. had to wait until a more appropriate time (which means after family time, bedtime, and me time—not necessarily in that order).

On Father's Day, for example, I tend to celebrate by taking my child to the zoo. For my birthday, the greatest gift that I could ever receive is the one that I give to myself: an entire day of fun and laughter with my little one, whether it is at an amusement park or in our living room. Furthermore, as a busy professional and entrepreneur, I make it a point to include my family in travel plans and coordinate trips to the amusement park or children's museum around business-related events. Just as importantly, I have developed an ironclad policy of mentally leaving my work at the doorstep prior to entering the sacred space of my home, understanding that nothing in the world can be as important as what's going on underneath the roof of my own home.

Moreover, as my children grow up and ultimately leave home one day, I want them to know beyond a shadow of a doubt that their father loved them and cherished the moments he had to spend with them each day.

### Rearview Glance: "Finding Izaiah"

In the 1995 film *Losing Isaiah*, two women from very opposite sides of the tracks find themselves embroiled in a gut-wrenching and nasty dispute for custody of a young boy. The boy, named Isaiah, was abandoned by his mother on a trash heap when he was but an infant. Academy Award-winning actress Halle Berry plays the destitute and miserable mother who is addicted to crack cocaine. She mistakenly abandons her son in a cardboard box next to a trash pile outside of a crack house while in a drug induced stupor. Upon realizing her grave and tragic mistake, Berry's character, Khailia Richards, rushes back to the crack den the very next morning. However, she arrives only to find her child gone, having been rescued by sanitation workers. Several years later, after Isaiah is adopted by another family, Richards seeks to regain custody of her child, having gone through rehab and cleaned up her act. She discovers that getting him back to be much more difficult than losing him.

After the death of my brother Bryant, he became a father, albeit posthumously. Sadly, the bouncing baby boy named Izaiah would never know his dad. After that enormously tragic event in my life, as my brother lay in his casket and I bid farewell, I promised him that I would always be a presence in the lives of his kids. As a 20-something bachelor, I never had the opportunity to fulfill that commitment. In fact, I could barely feed myself. But now, as a stable and successful family man who owns his own businesses and makes a decent income, I have no excuse for not doing something.

Nearly 15 years after Izaiah's birth, I traveled back home to eulogize my great-grandfather who lived a long and prosperous 94 years. At the time I certainly never realized that I would come home to the opportunity to fulfill a final commitment.

Immediately following my grandfather's funeral, a young woman approached me to introduce herself as the mother of my deceased brother's son. I had known about her but hadn't seen her in over a dozen years. Izaiah's mother, who started out as a teenaged parent, had more than bettered her situation—having earned both an undergraduate degree and master's degree, and was on her way to her doctorate. As a teacher striving to move into the upper echelons of school administration, she spoke to me of the importance of her child, my nephew, understanding that unless he aimed for college and beyond, he may very well be headed down the same self-destructive path his father traveled. As such, she suggested that I reconnect with Izaiah at this most critical stage in his life.

"He really needs some guidance and direction from someone close to him who has seen the other side of life," she said.

"Well, you know, when does he go back to school?" I inquired, as it was nearing the end of summer and the new school year was rapidly approaching.

"Three weeks."

"Tell you what," I said, "I'm going to buy him a plane ticket next week. Tell him he's going to spend a week with my family and me at our home in New York City."

Approximately ten days later, a gangly young man with a quiet disposition flew over 1,200 miles to spend a week with another side of himself that he had never really known. As this nearly 6-foot teenager strutted down the concourse at John F. Kennedy International Airport, looking every bit like his father's son, I stood there flummoxed, hardly believing what I was seeing. *My God, I feel like I'm looking at a ghost!* I thought to myself as he smiled and waved at me, having recognized my obvious recognition of him. This kid was literally the spitting image of an individual whom, the last time I saw him, I was putting in the ground at the Palm Beach Memorial Gardens Cemetery.

In his heartfelt song, "Dance With My Father," the late Luther Vandross sang of a longing to reconnect with his deceased father one more time in this lifetime. I too, longed for one more opportunity to reconnect with my own brothers, to share with them feelings and emotions that I never expressed during the times that they were alive. While I will never live to experience that reunion, I was granted the privilege of the next best thing: the opportunity to share the love I had for them with their offspring.

So, there we were, headed from the airport and off to experience a week of bonding and friendship that probably impacted me more than it did my nephew. Not only did we tour New York City in grand style, but we spent time just having fun at a local water park. I also took him to my office because I wanted him to see—for himself—that anything is possible through hard work and perseverance.

The National Urban League, a large and historic American institution, a venerable organization that holds significant power and influence, has its principal offices on Wall Street. Its aim, to empower African-Americans and other individuals of color to "enter the social and economic mainstream," was one that I wanted my nephew to experience firsthand in an office filled with professional men and women who looked just like him. For many years, I served as special assistant and chief of staff for the president and chief executive officer of the League, the Honorable Marc H. Morial, the former popular two-term mayor of New Orleans, Louisiana. Mr. Morial's position had once been led by the likes of Whitney Young and Vernon Jordan. In this role I had the privilege of mixing and mingling with the people who run the world. While sitting in my office, my nephew marveled at photographs of me with such luminaries as Presidents George W. Bush, Bill Clinton, and Barack Obama, First Lady Barbara Bush, and television and film personalities Judge Joe Brown, actor Danny Glover, and others. More importantly, I wanted him to see that the world is bigger than the city he has grown up in and that there are options outside the fate that befell a man he never knew—his father.

One day during his visit, Izaiah and I traveled to Woodbury Commons, a huge outlet mall north of New York City, to take him on what was a ritual for me at the end of each summer: shopping for new school clothes. Part of the reason I did so, besides the obvious fact that I felt compelled to contribute in some small manner to the success of this child, is my belief that social status is not only important to teenagers but is also tied closely to their own identity and self-esteem. For teenagers, appearance is important. At Izaiah's age, the way young people view themselves is often directly viewed through the prism of how other people view them. Helping him avoid the unnecessary distractions associated with decreased self-esteem and social ostracism simply because of his wardrobe was, for me, not an option.

Woodbury Commons has a number of high-end stores, including the Gap, Reebok, J. Crew, Banana Republic, and others. "You've got a $500 budget," I announced to a very surprised young man who could hardly believe his ears. A dozen stores later, one very exhausted teenager left the mall with a suitcase filled with new shoes, slacks, jeans, shirts, and undergarments. And though it made me feel good to do so, I don't deserve any measure of credit for my actions. It was what I was supposed to do.

And that has given me the license to live freely.

## Universal Road Rule: "Each One Reach One"

Before being used by the George W. Bush Administration, the phrase "Leave No Child Behind" was coined by Marian Wright Edelman of the Children's Defense Fund. The group, whose aim is to provide a quality life and equal opportunities for all children, developed the mantra as a means of communicating its overarching message of hope and opportunity for some of the most vulnerable members of society. Today, as we strive to make the communities we call home better places in which to live and learn, understanding the importance of being a productive, contributing member of society cannot be ignored. Mentorship is a means by which we all can impact our collective future. Moreover, the importance of giving back to others, both within our families and within our communities, cannot be overstated.

A passage from my favorite book says, *"Give, and it shall be given unto you; good measure, pressed down, and shaken together, and running over, shall men give into your bosom..."* (Luke 6:38). In laymen's terms, "If you give with a good heart, expecting nothing in return, be prepared for an overflow of blessings to come your way." As a believer in universal laws and principles, I am a witness to the power and efficacy of The Law of Reciprocity: "You reap what you sow" (see Gal. 6:7). If you plant corn during planting season, you can surely expect corn during harvest time. If you give, know that good things are just waiting to happen for you.

As the saying goes, "I never saw a person stand so tall as when they stooped to help a child." As a leader within your own right, there is no more important way to show that you are indeed invested in your community than by first being a role model to the children in your own life, whether you are a parent or not. Then, take the time to be a role model for a child in your neighborhood. Countless boys and girls have no positive influence within their lives to tell them right from wrong and to model leadership in the flesh through love, patience, and understanding. Some of these children may be living right next door to you, playing on your street, or being educated in your local schoolhouse. Just one hour a week can make a world of difference to those who are in need of a helping hand.

Although I did not have a father who cared enough to spend even an hour a week with me, my mother had the foresight and wisdom to understand that she couldn't raise her children alone. My siblings and I were enrolled, at an early age, in the Big Brothers Big Sisters of America program. It provided the guidance and camaraderie we needed with a responsible male influence in our lives. Mama understood that she couldn't teach her boys how to be men, and that's where extended family members, friends, and Big Brothers came in. Though this wonderful, life-changing program made a marked difference in my early development, it took more than six years before they were able to find a match for me because the volunteers simply weren't there.

In their book, *What's God Got to Do With the American Experiment?*, authors E.J. Dionne and John J. Diulio underscore the all-too-important role that community groups and mentors can have on the lives of those children who have been left behind.

> Day by day, clergy, volunteers and people of faith monitor, mentor and minister to the daily needs of the inner city black children who, through no fault of their own, live in neighborhoods where opportunities are few and drugs, crime and failed public schools are common. There, faith driven community activists strive against the odds to help these children...[10]

As a child growing up in the Christian tradition, it was always impressed upon me that, even when it seems as if there is no way out of a terrible situation, "God always has a ram in the bush." Not having a father's presence in my life, that lifeline for me was Big Brothers Big Sisters of America.

For over 100 years, Big Brothers and Big Sisters have worked to help young men and women become productive and well-adjusted members of society through an innovative one-to-one mentorship program that has proven to work and has been enormously successful. Each year hundreds of thousands of children, "Littles," are matched with caring adult volunteers, "Bigs," in a mentorship arrangement that changes the lives of all parties involved. Research has found that the program offers a comprehensive initiative "that focuses less on specific problems after they occur, and more on meeting youths' most basic developmental needs."[11] Having been a grateful beneficiary of this wonderful organization, I understand firsthand the impact that mentorship has on the life of a child. In following this mantra, I have committed myself to mentoring, assisting in whatever small measure that I can to help others achieve their own goals and dreams while prompting them to raise the expectations they have for themselves. In fact, since the deaths of my loved ones, I have helped similarly situated young black men better themselves and pursue their chosen fields of endeavor.

To that end, though I have my own responsibilities at home as a father and a friend, I made a promise to myself and my Creator, after the deaths of my brothers and cousins, young black men cut down before the prime of their lives: I would mentor at least one young person each year. Since then I have helped more than a dozen talented young men reach their full potential and strive to step into their own futures as leaders for the 21st century. I've served as a mentor, employer, coach, piggybank, housing bureau, big brother, and friend. Some of them have gone on to become lawyers, teachers, and community activists, and all have become contributing members of the community. While I may not have been able to prevent the loss of my own brothers, I can play some small but meaningful role in the lives of others who simply need someone to believe in them and help provide them with the opportunity they need to excel and succeed in life.

 ### Real Life Road Map: "Remember Your Roots"

The following action items are steps that you can take immediately to begin improving the quality of your life as you speed down the highways of life:

- Reclaim Your Birthright—Having been fearfully and wonderfully made in the image of the Creator, you were born with certain inalienable rights, among which are the freedom to choose a different course for yourself and a license to live the life that you deserve.

- Reaffirm your uniqueness in the world by first being true to yourself and the purpose to which you have been called to fulfill. First, this means taking an honest inventory of your character within and doing a self-check when you know you've come up wanting. "Know Thyself" has been one of life's truisms for several thousand years for a reason.

- Always remember that life itself is a privilege that can be revoked at anytime. Live full and die empty.

- Acknowledge Your Past—Denying the experiences that are uniquely your own will only delay the very real and necessary healing you will need before you can successfully traverse the twists and turns of life.

- Confront the negative ghosts of your past and drop off, along the side of the road, any excess baggage holding you back and slowing you down as you drive into your future.

- Embrace the obstacles you have overcome in life as lessons learned and opportunities to turn challenges into triumphs.

- Leave No Child Behind—As a committed member of the human race, we all have a personal responsibility to help uplift the lives of the "least of these" by giving of our time, talents, and treasure to better the lives of our community's children.

- Spend quality time with the children in your life and let them know on a regular basis how important they are both to you and the world they will inherit as adults.

- Sign up with Big Brothers Big Sisters of America or another reputable mentorship organization and spend one hour a week mentoring a child.

Chapter 2

# STUDY TO SHOW YOURSELF APPROVAL

NOTED GREEK philosopher Antisthenes once observed, "The investigation of the meaning of words is the beginning of education." Throughout history, continuing and advanced education has played a vital role in the development of society and the advancement of those fortunate enough to receive an education, as well as for their posterity. Having acquired a thirst for knowledge at a very early age, education has always been stressed as the key to transforming my existence and changing my economic circumstances for the better. As such, I have frequently been forced to swim upstream against a current of poor educational options. This had the potential to leave me languishing in a sea of hopelessness and despair, were it not for a few committed teachers who endeavored to see me succeed in spite of my challenges.

Preparing to get a driver's license is much the same way. It's a time-consuming process that requires diligent study and preparation before we are allowed to get on the road. Proper preparation is a prerequisite for safe operation—whether in a vehicle or in the driver's seat of life. In the game of life, studying is a requirement for professional and personal success and is essential to the human soul. This section will explore the importance of education for our individual development.

## STOP Red Light Challenge: "He Act Like He White"

"He act like he white," I often heard as I strived to excel and succeed through the formative years of my education process. For a young black man growing up in a relatively oppressive environment, any sign of assimilation into mainstream society was seen as a rejection of one's "blackness" and a clear indication that I was "not down" for the cause. In such a setting, I often found myself ostracized and ridiculed by my peers who found hanging out in the hallways much more palatable than paying attention in class. As an individual who holds enormous pride in his heritage and ancestry, the label I received at the hands of so-called "friends" was wounding in its impact, yet it helped to strengthen my resolve to prove to my detractors that smart people came in all shapes, sizes, and colors. Race, in my opinion, had nothing to do with one's capacity to learn, and I was bound and determined to prove it.

In his essay "The Cult of Anti-Intellectualism Amongst Blacks," author Walter Williams observed:

>...Black anti-intellectualism is a result of victimology and separatism. Black politicians, civil-rights leaders and white liberals have peddled victimhood to black youngsters, teaching them that racism is pervasive and no amount of individual effort can overcome racist barriers.[1]

According to most available statistics, black students consistently underperform their white and Asian counterparts in academic tests and graduation rates, leaving generations of students further and further behind in the race to simply catch up to the rest of the world. In fact, nearly three-quarters of all African-American college students fail to have earned their degrees five years after entering undergraduate school. I believe this is due, in no small measure, to the pervasive attitude amongst many in my race who believe that "thug life" is preferable to college life.

Sadly, many of those black students who are afforded the privilege to receive a post-secondary education often spend their time on campus skipping classes and performing poorly on tests. They sometimes lament their academic travails as the fault of racist teachers and unfair grading practices, while hardly ever acknowledging their own mistakes.

> ...Racial discrimination is not the major problem for blacks today. Instead, it's self-sabotage...Black students have the nation's lowest academic achievement. That can't be blamed on racism because academic achievement is the lowest in cities where the mayor, superintendent of schools, and most principals and teachers are black, such as Washington, D.C., Philadelphia and Detroit...[2]

Having left my alma mater, Hampton University, a semester shy of graduation after the deaths of my brothers, I have come to appreciate very much my own educational experience—one that has taught me the importance of seeing my goals through to the end and never giving up. During this trying time in my life, one of the hardest things that I ever had to do was to leave my beloved alma mater not having received my diploma. My grade point average had hit rock bottom due in a large extent to the fact that I was suffering from enormous grief that would confound the imagination. I left the university and worked several dead-end jobs, being paid a pittance of my fair market value simply because I had no degree. "We would like to pay you more, Elvin. As soon as you get your degree, let us know and we will reexamine your situation," is what I was often confronted with whenever I asked for a raise.

As a result of these repeated rejections for more pay and authority on the job, I soon came to learn that "talent and fifty cents may get you a cup of coffee." And, after the advent of Starbucks and Seattle's Best Coffee, I soon learned that even that was a stretch! You see, having not completed my formal education, I came to realize the hard way that my skills and capabilities were no match, in the corporate arena, for having a Bachelor's degree. In the words of Sir Arthur Helps, "Nothing succeeds like success," and that is, indeed, the gospel truth when it comes to an individual's perceived value in the workforce.

Nearly six years after leaving Hampton University, my "home by the sea," I eventually earned a Bachelor of Science Degree in Social Science, with a minor in Government and Politics from the University of Maryland. Additionally, as a candidate for a Master of Professional Studies degree in Ministry from the New York Theological Seminary and the recipient of several professional industry certifications, I am all the more grateful for having crossed this academic threshold. Most importantly, it is an example to my own child that continuing education is critical to success. I sacrificed the basic necessities to pay for school on my own, without the assistance of financial aid or scholarships. And I ultimately finished each semester in both undergraduate and graduate school on the Dean's list, refusing to earn any poor grades on my own dime.

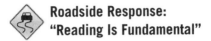 ## Roadside Response: "Reading Is Fundamental"

In a letter to his young protégé, Timothy, the apostle Paul of the Christian tradition admonished the young man to:

> *Study and be eager and do your utmost to present yourself to God approved (tested by trial), a workman who has no cause to be ashamed, correctly analyzing and accurately dividing [rightly handling and skillfully teaching] the Word of Truth* (2 Timothy 2:15 AMP).

As a young boy I came to find these words to be a road map for my own success. I will never forget the first time I was exposed to a book fair as a second grade student at the Westward Elementary School in West Palm Beach, Florida. R.I.F., short for "Reading Is Fundamental," is America's oldest and largest nonprofit children's literacy organization, bringing low cost books to children of all economic backgrounds. As a result of my exposure to R.I.F., my love of learning was stoked all the more through the likes of Judy Blume's *Super Fudge*, as well as the *Hardy Boys Series*. These books inspired me to discover a world I had previously never known, hidden within the covers of fascinating books. Having been reared in a family that stressed educational advancement, the most fundamental experience in my personal development was the summer that I learned how to read, when I was 4 years old. What's so memorable about this experience, however, is that it was punctuated by the sting of a long wooden ruler, which was swung into action by my older cousin, Marsha' McClendon, every time I got a word wrong.

Before I continue, let me just say that my cousin Marsha', who gave me the gift of reading, used tactics and tools that were publicly acceptable and available to her in the late 1970s—but boy, those tactics hurt! She taught me, however, in no uncertain terms, that if I wanted to be successful in the game of life, then reading was my first priority. She reminded me that people had suffered and died to learn a necessary skill that so many still take for granted. This, she explained, would be my big ticket out of the ghetto, but first I had to go through Bugs Bunny to prove it. In one week's time she taught me to read and, in doing so, unveiled a new world of possibilities that would literally change my future.

*Bugs Bunny Goes to Space*, a comedic short story about the antics of the venerable king of cartoon was, as my cousin would falsely lull me to believe, an exciting book to read. However, *exciting* was not the word that I would use to describe what unfolded. As I would soon find out, for every word that I did not comprehend, I had to extend my hand for a severe and painful thrashing. (I'm talking smack down, baby! Well... maybe not that bad, but you get the point.) After fumbling around my newfound vocabulary minefield, I learned to read in the course of a few days and haven't looked back since.

From that point forward, I couldn't get enough. I read everything from the daily newspaper to constitutional law books at 6 years old, daydreaming that one day maybe I could be the first black president of the United States of America! (Well, we all know how that turned out. You snooze, you lose, I guess.) I am grateful for the fire that my cousin lit in my heart (and the flames that wooden ruler sparked on my hand as well). Now I understand wholeheartedly what my mentor, the late Dr. William Malcolm Batts III, meant when he so often declared: "No one can save us for us but us. If it is to be, it's up to me." Moreover, as a proud father of a black and Latino son, I want to impart to him the gift that my cousin gave to me, minus the ruler of course. Then he, too, will be prepared to react to the pitch when life throws him a curve ball. If it worked for me, it will work for him.

Today, as I reflect upon this formidable educational experience, I lament, in despair, the fate of Generation Y and those who will come behind them. They are often portrayed as doing nothing but reading text messages all day and speaking in coded shorthand, leaving them woefully unprepared for the future. *(Fast-forward some three decades after my learning to read.)* Having served on the board of trustees of one of the nation's leading charter schools, I have been placed in a position of being able to impact affirmatively the lives of little children who remind me so much of myself when I was their age. The Harlem Success Academy in New York City, a network of free, public elementary schools, was established on a simple premise: "Every child can succeed." A public school run like a private school, the school's "Success Scholars" are taught by the best and brightest teachers from around the country, who track each student's personal progress every eight weeks. Those who require additional assistance are provided one-to-one tutoring by highly trained tutors to ensure they don't fall into the chasm we have come to know as the "achievement gap." Harlem Success' mission of ensuring that every student graduates from college is not just laudable but one that can be realized if each of us within the educational network—parents, teachers, students, administrators, and members of the concerned community—develop an "academic village" in each of our schools to help raise and educate our children.

To that end, I am an ardent supporter of early childhood education, longer school days, an expanded school year, and academic enrichment courses for all of America's children to provide them with a well-rounded education. As a member of the board of trustees for Harlem Success, I served as an unyielding advocate for both students and parents, ensuring that their needs were of the most paramount importance. Additionally, I strived to participate in the academic life of the students while fighting to make sure that the practical needs of the families from which they hailed were addressed. Today, I continue to work to provide educational equality for the "least of these." I aim, in some small way, to counteract the negative academic trends facing not just blacks but all those who don't have access to or do not fully appreciate a quality education. ("If not me, then who? If not now, then when?")

### Rearview Glance: "Spell Zucchini"

Growing up as a child, I was often one of a few black students who were placed in advanced learning classes and who participated in the school's spelling bees. More often than not, I was teased by my fellow black students as "acting white" because I actually enjoyed school and the opportunity to learn new things. Nonetheless, I ignored the naysayers who knew not what they spoke of and ventured into the realm of activities that promoted intellectual stimulation and learning far beyond the classroom setting. In fact, one year I even won the school spelling bee and placed first runner up at the county level for the countywide bee sponsored by *The Palm Beach Post*.

I can remember it just like it was yesterday, as the numbers dwindled to ten and then five and then three. There I was, still standing, when it finally came down to two spellers: a worthy opponent whom I immediately sized up as easy to beat, and myself. Then came my Waterloo.

"Please spell 'zucchini.'"

"Zoo who?"

"Zucchini."

"May I have that in a sentence?" I asked. The truth is, I was stalling for time. I had studied the spelling bee "Book of Words" provided by the local newspaper every day, every opportunity I had. But I didn't get to the Zs! Now, I had to wing it. "Z-o-o-k-i-n-y. Zookiny!?" Boy was I wrong!

"I'm sorry, that is incorrect."

And just like that, my dreams of a free trip to the state competition and onto the Scripps Howard National Spelling Bee were dashed.

What I did get from that experience has continued to last a lifetime. First, I got a thirst for words and their etymologies and the ability to utilize them in a sentence, believing my English teachers who reminded me that if I use a word in a sentence three times, it was mine forever. Second, I learned that if you run a race, go all the way until the end. You see, in my spelling bee debacle, I studied the "Book of Words" assiduously, all the way to the Xs, thinking, *Surely this thing will be over long before they get to the Zs*. Once again, I had miscalculated and would be handed an opportunity to begin again more intelligently, as I didn't study all the way until the end. It was only then that I understood what the author of Ecclesiastes 9:11 meant with these words: *"The race is not given to the swift, nor the battle to the strong, but he that endures to the end."*

 ### Universal Road Rule: "The Early Bird Gets the Worm"

Famed black nationalist minister Malcolm X once intoned: "Education is our passport to the future, for tomorrow belongs to the people who prepare for it today." As the world becomes smaller and smaller and the barriers of geography, language, and race continue to dissolve away to make room for expanded global commerce and trade, education has become the most important ingredient in an individual's formula for success. Can one make it to the top of society in terms of economic and social advancement without a college degree? Yes. Is it an easy feat to accomplish? No. What is important to remember, nonetheless, is that college preparation starts at the pre-school level where a child's first classroom is: at home.

Nearly five months after the birth of my child, my wife and I began teaching him how to read using an innovative program called *Your Baby Can Read*®. An early language development system that helps to increase the communication skills, enhance learning ability, and provide greater confidence to young children between the ages of birth and 5 years old, this unique program produces astonishing results in children. Assisting them in preparing for entry to grade school, *Your Baby Can Read* is, for many people, an antidote to the educational neglect that takes place in a child's life prior to ever entering a classroom. It starts by teaching them how to read, write, and comprehend.

Moreover, as crime continues to skyrocket out of control, empowering our children with the skills that they need to be self-sufficient individuals is becoming even more important. The United States continues to expand its "Cradle to Prison Pipeline" wherein poor-performing students, more often than not, end up as hardened criminals and prisoners in state penal institutions. The need to combat this downward spiral has become an important indicator in the direction our future generations are heading. According to data extracted from various state Departments of Corrections, they literally plan their budgets around the success or failure of the children in the public schools. California, for example, has seen an increase in its prison population of over 800% just between the years 1978 and 1998. If a child is not reading at proficiency level by the time they reach the fourth grade in California, the state begins planning to receive that child as a long-term guest of its penal system. Arizona starts assessing their prison population by looking at third grade scores, and some states start as early as grade two. To combat this issue, which has already become an enormous drain on taxpayer resources, the onus is on us as citizens who care about our society to do whatever we can to reverse this negative trend.

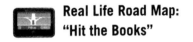

### Real Life Road Map: "Hit the Books"

The following action items are steps that you can take immediately to begin improving the quality of your life as you speed down the highways of life:

- Study hard—It has often been said that hard work never killed anybody. A vigorous course of continuing academic study, whether in school or at home, is important for the up-building of the mind and a nation.

- Develop a regular course of study that provides a continuing education program for both yourself and those you love by acquiring books that spark your interests.

- Set aside at least 15 minutes every day to stimulate your mind by reading something of educational value and content.

- Reject labels—It doesn't matter what others call you, it's what you answer to that counts. When confronting the challenges of ignorance and negativity that aim to keep you in darkness, rejecting those sentiments early and often is critical in helping you to overcome external adversity.

- Consider the source of your ridicule and how well they have turned out. You can, and must, do better!

- Always remember—"Sticks and stones may break your bones but names will never hurt you."

- Start early—Record producer John Hammond once said: "The early bird gets the worm, but the second mouse gets the cheese." As parents and concerned community citizens, preparing all of our children early by teaching them the fundamentals of reading, writing, and arithmetic *before* they report to kindergarten is critical to each student's future success.

- Inspire a love of learning in the hearts of the children in your life by taking the time to read to them.

- Get involved in your local educational system by participating in Parent-Teacher Associations, volunteering at your local school, or supporting educational enrichment activities sponsored by well-meaning groups and organizations with your time, talent, and treasure.

## Find Good Teachers and Avoid Bad Ones

French poet and novelist Anatole France once observed, "The whole art of teaching is only the art of awakening the natural curiosity of young minds for the purpose of satisfying it afterwards."[3] Throughout my secondary education as I matriculated through school, I was fortunate to have dedicated and committed teachers who were faithful to their life's mission of impacting the lives of young people in meaningful and demonstrable ways. One such individual, Mr. Eric B. Bailey, an older Caucasian man, saw in me, a young black boy, a leader just waiting to emerge. He made it his goal to help bring out my hidden potential. Each day at the beginning of class, Mr. Bailey would remind his students and have us recite in unison a mantra that I continue to espouse to this day: "Education means money. Money means power. And power means...more money!"

As the United States of America faces the most challenging economic times in generations, Mr. Bailey's insistent admonishment that we, as students, continue our quest for economic prosperity and financial freedom through our academic pursuits, has proven both to be correct and quite prescient. This is true even for me, a poor country boy from Florida. Perhaps he was looking through some sort of crystal ball all those many years ago, or he just understood that education itself was the great equalizer, and the higher we climbed the educational ladder the more achievable our dreams would become. Either way, Mr. Bailey was onto something way back when, even when I thought I already knew everything. "Go to college, Elvin," Mr. Bailey would say, "you're too smart to be stupid!" When I complained about being poor and not having the money to pay for college on my own, he would simply respond, "You see, Elvin, life just keeps going and going—warts and all—just live long enough." The better question, he reasoned, that I should ask myself was even simpler: "What am I going to do about it?"

 ### Red Light Challenge: "You'll Never Amount to Anything"

In the final scene of the critically acclaimed 1983 film *Teachers*, actor Nick Nolte, when told he was crazy for continuing to support students whom others had given up on, decried resolutely and succinctly: "I'm a teacher. I'm a teacher!" As a young man who was criticized by my own teachers for dreaming too big and not "staying in my place," I too have faced harsh criticism from those who should have been nothing but supportive of my positive goals and actions—my teachers. As such, I believe that it is vitally important to remember to avoid bad teachers who oftentimes impede your progress, waste your time, and wound your spirit with their words and deeds (or lack thereof). At the same time, identify the good teachers and latch onto them.

As student body president my senior year of high school, I was instrumental in achieving a number of milestones for my school that were notable in and of themselves. First, our student council was ranked by the National Association of Secondary School Principals as the number one student organization in the country during my tenure. Equally important, I helped to negotiate nearly $100,000 for the purchase of bleachers to erect on the school's football field, which hadn't seen a home game since we moved onto the new campus three years prior. You see, prior to this coup, our teams had been playing on a rival school's field because neither our home team nor our guests had any place to sit for the games on our campus. As celebrated as those achievements were, however, they were no match for the brutal facts: I was flunking math, and in order to graduate, I was going to have to go to summer school for the first time in my life. This may not have been so bad, except for the fact that I was the student body president! Talk about completely embarrassing! Here I am, Mr. "Man About Town" headed straight to summer school while my classmates headed straight across the graduation stage and onto the nearest beach.

To pour a bit of salt in an already festering wound, my Algebra II teacher, a middle-aged man with a prickly personality and a disdain for "all things Elvin," openly gloated that he had finally "cut the King of Campus" back down to size. According to his prediction, I would never amount to anything. Many years later I had the rare chance of seeing him again when I returned to my high school as a guest lecturer for a student assembly. I reminded him of his prognostication to those many years before. After initially feigning ignorance and pretending not to even know who I was, he simply walked away in disgust without so much as shaking my hand. In his simple act of defiance, I learned that some people, regardless of what you do, or simply because of who you are, will never acknowledge your gifts. My job was to use his ignorance to fuel my passion for uplifting the lives of "the least of these" through the power of my example. Was I upset with him? No. Tickled pink? Absolutely! But there is one thing I will always give him credit for: at least he was upfront about how he felt when I was his student...But God had the last word on that one—and He who laughs last, laughs best! Even still, I have come to develop and have enormous respect for those who boldly speak what is on their minds. For with them, I at least know where I stand. In the words of the noted French philosopher Voltaire: "I do not agree with what you have to say, but I will defend to the death your right to say it."

 ## Roadside Response: "Don't Become the Cream of the Crap"

Each day, from ninth through twelfth grade, I studied public speaking and parliamentary procedure in an unusual hybrid course of student government and debate our school called *Leadership Skills Development*. In this course, better known as Student Council to the 100 students who chose it as an elective credit each year, I learned how to conduct meetings using Robert's Rules of Order. I would later need this skill in a wide variety of activities in which I have found myself engaged throughout the years. I also learned how to pull the levers of power and manage them effectively as an elected leader representing the will and consent of the governed.

Moreover, I learned how to author bills and debate the merits of legislation. I perfected my skills at moving that legislation through committee, through various readings by the full chambers of each house within the student government, and eventually onto a final vote where the bill either passed or failed in each chamber of our exalted institution. To kill a bill before it had the opportunity to make it to the floor for an up or down vote, I learned the art of co-opting the members of the committee to vote down the legislation right there at the committee level. If that didn't work, I would utilize a little-known parliamentary trick known as "striking the enacting clause" of a bill, which would, essentially, stop the bill cold right there on the spot. Without the words "a bill to be enacted," nothing could happen. I knew this and would, from time to time, use it as a nuclear option when advancing a particular political agenda. Now mind you, I was 14 years old when this love affair with all things political and the actual nuances of making law took hold, but the lessons I learned would last me a lifetime. My skills were shaped on the floor of the Student Council room, where we literally built a grand podium and chambers out of the wood from the floor of an old dance studio. Ultimately my leadership skills were recognized as a model for management at the student level.

Another way I used what I had to get what I wanted was through my skills at oratory and an uncanny ability to connect with an audience though the soaring echoes of my voice in rhyme and cadence. *"How long...Not long!"* I would intone, invoking memories of the civil rights movement. In contest after contest, I swept the local oratorical competitions like Mike Tyson besting his opponents. Each summer during the various cultural arts festivals and every January at the advent of the Martin Luther King Jr. Day celebrations, I racked up hundreds of dollars in cash prizes, while honing my skills through speech composition and oral delivery. You see, I was somewhat of a ringer in those homespun competitions meant to inspire greatness from among the various candidates assembled to do a bit of verbal jousting.

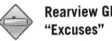 **Rearview Glance: "Excuses"**

"Elvin," Mr. Bailey would roar, "Do I have to stand up here and piss wooden nickels to get you to understand where I am coming from? As a black man in a white world, you are going to have to be twice as good to get half as far, and you'll need more degrees than a thermometer just to be taken seriously." While he may not have anticipated 20-plus years ago how much America would change in the age of Obama, Mr. Bailey was onto something—of that I am convinced. No one was going to give me anything free in this life, for anything worth having wasn't free anyway.

Many years later, I too would return to the classroom, this time as an instructor for extraordinarily talented minority high school students in an accelerated Saturday School program offered by Columbia University in New York City called the Double Discovery Program. I preached the same gospel of personal success Mr. Bailey taught to me: "Excuses are tools of the incompetent. They build monuments of nothingness and those who specialize in them seldom accomplish anything." Whatever your hurts, habits, and hang-ups—get over it. Life keeps on passing you by, and it sure isn't a dress rehearsal! Perhaps that's why I made a point on my 25th birthday to seek out my father, give him a great big hug, and let him know that I forgave him for what he didn't do for me. But most importantly, I forgave myself for holding onto the baggage he left in my life when he walked out the door of responsibility.

## Universal Road Rule: "It Takes a Village to Raise a Child"

In her book *It Takes a Village to Raise a Child*, United States secretary of state and former first lady, Hillary Rodham Clinton, borrowed the mantra from an ancient African proverb to underscore the importance of employing a community approach in helping watch our nation's children achieve their God-given potential.[4] Novelist and physician Robin Cook once said: "Education is more than a luxury; it is a responsibility that society owes to itself."[5] As committed members of our world community, everyone plays a role in the development of our children. Whether it is as parents, coaches, teachers, clergy, or just ordinary citizens who strive to make a difference, everyone can do something to make the world a better place through the eyes of a child.

Having spent a considerable amount of time as a motivational speaker in public schools around the country, I have come to experience firsthand the positive benefits that mentorship and volunteerism can have on young people. Moreover, I have witnessed it in my capacity as a Saturday School instructor in Columbia University's Double Discovery Center, which aims to give talented low-income students a helping hand as they strive to compete and win in a demanding global society. It was begun in the 1960s by Columbia students determined to make an impact upon the broader community outside of the confines of the university's hallowed halls. The program's mission is:

> To provide model educational programs and services which will enable young people historically underrepresented in higher education to pursue their highest aspirations and to achieve the full breadth of their intellectual potential. To instill the confidence, pride, curiosity and hope needed to complete secondary school, challenge oneself intellectually and embark on the path of higher education.[6]

As a teacher working for very little pay, I spent my Saturday mornings for months on end training some of the brightest young men and women New York has to offer. During that remarkable experience with the DDC students, I learned, perhaps, more from them than they did from me. I personally discovered that all children, when given an opportunity to succeed, can rise to the occasion and do extraordinary things with the proper guidance and a helping hand. In addition, I learned that I too was enriched by an experience that helped me to believe again in the future of our nation's youth.

I have heard it said, "Some rely on stocks and bonds in order to gain security—others invest in children's lives and are builders for eternity." As the architects of a brighter future, your presence matters in the life of a child. Taking the time to be an integral part of their lives is as important a civic duty as paying taxes. Without your involvement our future is imperiled; but with your engagement and support, the potential for achievement is limitless.

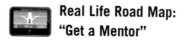

## Real Life Road Map: "Get a Mentor"

The following action items are steps that you can take immediately to begin improving the quality of your life as you speed down the highways of life:

- Find Good Teachers—In order for students to be inspired to greatness, it is important that parents and guardians, in consultation with their child, identify, early on, exceptional teachers and mentors who are committed to their personal achievement.

- Both parents and students should interview teachers, coaches, and mentors to determine their fitness for service and commitment to the personal success of the students they have been hired to educate and serve.

- Ignore Critics—There will be times in your life where those who may not be invested in your future attempt to rain on your parade. Like water and air, critics are always present and are very rarely in short supply. Allowing their negative expectations to penetrate your spirit is like putting water inside a boat and suddenly being surprised when it starts to sink. Negative thoughts, when internalized, produce negative results in our lives. Ignore them, as they mean you no good anyway!

- Mentorship Matters—The time that you spend mentoring young people within your community can be the missing link that students need to step into their greatness. Chances are, after all, that a teacher or mentor inspired you along the way. Mentorship is contagious—pass it on!

- Participate in Parent-Teacher Associations, student youth groups, and other organizations that help to build stronger schools and stronger communities.

Chapter 3

# IF AT FIRST YOU DON'T SUCCEED...

FAMED GOLFER Ben Hogan once declared: "Golf is like a game of luck. The more I play, the luckier I get." As we strive to get a license to live our dreams, understanding that success comes only after failure many times, the better we become at passing the test when the opportunity presents itself again. As an individual who has seen my fair share of losses, setbacks, and defeats, realizing that I will fall sometimes is critical to my success. More important, by admitting those failures, learning from them, and moving on to incorporate those stories into the fabric of my life, I have earned my own "license to live" again. And I believe that you can too. How often have you felt as if the world has simply passed you by? When was the last time you felt as if you were living your dreams? Whether that dream consists of frying chicken at the corner bodega, speaking in front of crowds of thousands, or simply taking the time to listen, you have an opportunity to turn it around, understanding that you truly can make it. As a young college initiate of the Alpha Phi Alpha Fraternity, Inc., I learned a number of poems and songs that continue to give me strength in tough times today. One of them was a poem I often recited, including this often-quoted gem I remember to this day: "Failure is the opportunity to begin again more intelligently. It is a temporary obstacle in the quest towards the light that I must learn to hurdle no matter the consequences or pain."[1]

In layman's terms, it's OK to mess up sometimes—as long as you keep on keeping on. In fact, that's how success stories are made. It has often been said, "Failure is not the worst thing in the world. The very worst thing is not to try." As you strive to step into your greatness, it is important to remember that failure is nothing but the perfect chance to start all over again.

For thirty years, the Washington Redskins competed for Super Bowl glory, in hopes of winning a championship for the pride of the nation's capitol to call its own. Not once had they been successful in their efforts until, in 1972, now legendary Coach George Allen exhorted them to reach within themselves to achieve a miracle. "Just remember. Forty men together can't lose," he reminded his team before they took to the gridiron. That day, in spite of thirty years of defeats and thirty years of dashed hopes, the Redskins won the NFC Championship against their bitter rivals, the Cowboys, in a victory that will never be forgotten.

According to statistics from that day's game, it took the Cowboys over twenty minutes to record a first down on a day that—legend has it—belonged to the Redskins. "Nursing a 10-3 lead, quarterback Billy Kilmer hit Hall-of-Fame receiver Charley Taylor with a memorable 45-yard touchdown strike on the period's first play that drew the curtains on the Cowboys and sealed a win that ended with Allen being carried off the field."[2] The lesson in all of this is twofold. First, we must always remember that it takes five fingers to make up a hand and when clenched, a hand can form a mighty fist. It's easier getting to where you want to go when you work together—in unison—with others. Secondly, and just as important, regardless of how many times you experience defeat, you should never—ever—give up. You, too, have what it takes to be a champion—if only you just believe!

 ### Red Light Challenge: "Find an Empty Lot"

In driving down the highways of life, it is important to remember that "nothing beats a failure but a comeback!" The great American inventor Thomas Edison went through thousands of iterations of the light bulb before he came up with one that worked. Colonel Sanders went through dozens of versions of his famous recipe before he settled on eleven winning herbs and spices. Babe Ruth spent his childhood years in an orphanage and, as a baseball player, struck out 1,330 times on his way to the Hall of Fame. Elvis Presley was banished from the Grand Ole Opry after one performance and told: "You ain't goin' nowhere, son." This was before he became the King of Rock and Roll. Even Oprah Winfrey was fired from her television reporter's job and advised: "You're not fit for TV." Can you say Billion Dollar Baby?

Author Rudyard Kipling once said, "We have forty million reasons for failure, but not a single excuse." As a young college student I pledged as a member of Alpha Phi Alpha Fraternity, Inc., and the first poem we were required to learn was entitled "Excuses." I still remember it to this day: "Excuses are tools of incompetence. They build monuments of nothingness. Those who specialize in them seldom accomplish anything." When an individual first learns how to drive, they look for an empty lot or someplace isolated—with enough breathing room to make a few mistakes. (At least, that's what I did.) Not accepting excuses from myself, even when I knowingly do the wrong thing, also helps me to live a life of freedom from the shackles of manacled indecision.

Many say that, in life, "Failure is not an option." Today I would like to revise that statement to "Continuing in failure is not an option." I strive to capitalize on my mistakes to build a better mousetrap. As a child growing up in the "cold, cruel" South, my empty lot was a little church in the 'hood that taught a fundamental understanding of what it takes to have a strong spiritual foundation. "There's no street like 5th Street," was the slogan we used to describe our church family at the 5th Street Church of God and, for me, that was truth. I spent nearly six days a week in some form of church activity, whether it was Sunday service, Monday night Prayer Meeting, or Wednesday night Bible Study. During those formative years as a child and young teenager, I even earned a license in discipleship at the age of 16. Since then I have continued my thirst for knowledge and understanding, all the way to the New York Theological seminary where I have completed my Master's degree work in ministry. My godparents, Eddie and Bertha Dukes, took me every Sunday before I began to go by choice, and I learned the fundamentals of human decency and love for all mankind. Just as importantly, my church experience helped to shape my development for years to come and set me on a path toward my destiny of service to all as a friend of God and man. With this firm foundation and a need to fill the void left by the lack of a father and the loss of brothers, I joined the oldest black Greek letter organization in existence today, the Alpha Phi Alpha Fraternity, Inc., known for "manly deeds, scholarship, and love for all mankind."

### Roadside Response: "Get a New Group"

Often, when traveling along the highways of life, we find ourselves going with the flow of traffic. Part of having a license to operate on the highway presumes that you have the ability as a driver to not be an obstruction in traffic. What we must remember, however, is that getting ahead of ourselves, or lulling ourselves into a sense of security when speeding down the road, can often lead to our being fined or possibly detained for failure to obey the rules of the road.

Dr. Dennis Kimbro, author of *Think and Grow Rich: A Black Perspective*, once observed: "If you're the smartest person in your group, it's time to get yourself a new group!" In fact, I would venture to say that the way to transcend the space and place that you are in right now and go to the next level is by surrounding yourself with those who are where you want to be. My mother always taught me that "birds of a feather flock together." *(Does anybody live on my street?)* This can be achieved by joining professional groups within the industry in which you work, participating in seminars and workshops that attract like-minded individuals, or embarking on your own rigorous course of study that helps you to become an expert in your chosen field of endeavor. In Law 11 of *The 21 Irrefutable Laws of Leadership*, Dr. John C. Maxwell observes in the Law of the Inner Circle, "The potential of a leader—along with the potential of the whole organization—is determined by those closest to him."[3] In her time-honored poem, "Two Kinds of People," Ella Wheeler Wilcox, wrote:

There are two kinds of people on earth today.
Just two kinds of people, no more I say.

Not the good and the bad, for 'tis well understood,
that the good are half bad and the bad are half good…
No! The two kinds of people on earth, I mean—
are the people who lift and the people who lean.[4]

One of the immutable facts I learned early on and have remembered throughout my life is that you can't get through life alone. No matter what you are going through, having someone there to support you is important in your securing the brass ring you are so destined for. Seek the association of like-minded individuals who are doing better than you are right now and are where you want to be.

 ### Rearview Glance: "Crossing the Burning Sands"

Besides losing my brothers to tragic deaths and enduring my share of valleys, pledging Alpha as a scared 19-year-old kid was the toughest thing I ever did. Initiated through the auspices of the Gamma Iota chapter at Hampton University in Hampton, Virginia, the fraternity has been, for me, a place where service and brotherhood go hand in hand. This allows me, in turn, to be a better human being as I strive to uplift my community. At the start of the 20th century, black students at American universities were often excluded from the personal and close associations the predominantly white student population enjoyed in fraternal organizations. In his historic work *The History of Alpha Phi Alpha, a Development in College Life*, Dr. Charles Harris Wesley notes:

During the 1905–06 school year, predominantly white Cornell University saw the organization of the first Greek letter fraternity for black students, by black students. Alpha Phi

Alpha was organized with the stated aim to provide a mechanism to build those associations and provide mutual support among African American students.[5]

Founded on the Cornell campus in Ithaca, New York, Alpha Phi Alpha was formed out of a need for common brotherhood and mutual survival in a hostile northeastern collegiate environment at the turn of the 20th century. As an impressionable young man who wanted to belong, I was immediately drawn to the Alphas and their desire to uplift the lives of the "least of these" through leadership by example. They served the community with earnestness and devotion, and boasted some of the world's foremost black leaders—the captains of power and industry who refused to allow overwhelming odds to stop them from achieving their goals.

As number one in my line of 19 "Line Brothers" who hailed from varying and disparate backgrounds and communities, I was not only the shortest guy in the group, I was also the first to endure whatever fate befell us. I had to do so with courage and conviction so that my peers would have heart and be strong. One time, during a particularly arduous task of entertaining our "Big Brothers," I performed an unusual skit that would soon give my line a free pass to a night closer to hell, granting us a reprieve from our impending doom. After forgetting the line to a particular poem, one of my line brothers faltered and stumbled as he struggled to regain his footing. Suddenly, I broke into my best rendition of Carlton Banks from "The Fresh Prince of Bel-Air" performing Tom Jones' "It's Not Unusual":

*It's not unusual to be loved by anyone.*
*It's not unusual to have fun with anyone*
*But when I see you hanging about with anyone,*

*It's not unusual to see me cry...*
*Oh, I wanna' die.*

By the time I was finished crooning to my heart's content, my brothers were in stitches and the entire room had burst into an uncontrollable laughter that went on for several minutes.

I learned from that experience that it is important to remember to use levity at times to lighten a situation and spark joy in times of trouble. As we strive to earn our own license to live, using laughter in times of failure can help to bolster our efforts the next time around when we get up again.

 ## Universal Road Rule:
## "Don't Forget Where You Come From"

One of the easiest things for a wayward traveler to do when he (or she) takes his eyes off his goal is to forget from whence he came. When you become a member of the gentrified class, be sure to do as the Romans do, but never forget where you came from... After all, "If you don't know where you are going, any road will take you there."

Many people make it to what they believe to be the Promised Land only to forget those left back in Egypt. I would venture to say the sin of forgetting those left behind is one of the most egregious and deserves particular recognition.

Speaking of forgetting, I am reminded of an 80-year-old couple who were having problems remembering things, so they decided to go to their doctor to get checked out. When they arrived at the doctor's office, they explained the problems they were having with their memories. After checking the couple out, the doctor told them that they were fine physically but should start writing things down and making notes to help them remember things. Soon after, back at home, the old man gets up from his chair and his wife asks, "Where are you going?"

He replies, "To the kitchen to get me some ice cream."

"Will you bring me some too?" she asks.

"Sure."

She then asks him, "Don't you think you should write it down so you don't forget?"

"No, I can remember that," he says.

She replies, "Put strawberries on top."

He yells back, "I can remember that you want a bowl of ice cream with strawberries."

"Well, I also would like whipped cream on top. I know you will forget that so you better write it down."

Now a bit exasperated, the old man responds: "I don't need to write that down, I can remember that." He then fumes into the kitchen. After about 20 minutes he returns and hands her a plate of ham and eggs.

She looks at the plate, looks at him, looks back at the plate, and says: "See, I knew you would forget the toast."

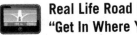 ## Real Life Road Map: "Get In Where You Fit In"

As mentioned, I joined a fraternal organization that strived to make a difference, with a strict list of prerequisites that one must achieve to be considered a part of the number. But in addition to being an Alpha man, I also understood that being myself was paramount to my living a life of full acceptance of who and what I am destined to become. As you strive to earn your credentials, maintaining your sense of self is important to become the person you are meant to be.

Joining new and forward-thinking organizations can also be beneficial to your bottom line. Most professional organizations keep up-to-date job banks that list opportunities submitted by employers and organization members. It's a good place for employers to advertise if they're in the market for someone who is skilled and qualified because joining a professional organization shows intelligence, commitment, and a willingness to seek and share knowledge. Moreover, employers often simply pick up the phone and call professional associations to ask for recommendations for job openings. "Get in where you fit in" on the highways of life as you ease on down the road.

 ### Red Light Challenge: "Practice, Practice, Practice..."

If a man is called to be a street sweeper, he should sweep streets even as Michelangelo painted, or Beethoven played music, or Shakespeare wrote poetry. He should sweep streets so well that all the hosts of heaven and earth will pause to say, "Here lived a great street sweeper who did his job well."[6]

These words, spoken by the Rev. Dr. Martin Luther King Jr., help to underscore the importance of doing a job well. Malcolm Gladwell reminds us in his book, *Outliers: The Story of Success*, that "Practice isn't the thing you do once you're good. Practice is the thing you do that makes you good."[7] Throughout childhood I honed my oratory skills by participating in and winning competitive contests. Success in life, in my opinion, is directly attributable to how good you are at what you do best.

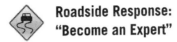

## Roadside Response: "Become an Expert"

Gladwell uncovered the underlying commonality between those who succeed and those who do not: sheer commitment. "It takes 10,000 hours to become a world class expert—at anything."[8] To become an expert at anything is going to take some time for practice, but once you achieve the status of expert, the only person who can change that status is you. As a young man who discovered my gift of communication early on in life, I honed my innate skills through oratorical competitions, essay contests, and team debates that helped to shape my talents into an ability to uplift the lives of the least of these and those who are in need.

Since that time, I have worked to improve upon those skills by participating in workshops, seminars, and training events. These help to bring out the best in me by building upon the skills that I have already developed while teaching me new skills that I can add to a growing catalog of communications abilities. Additionally, one of the habits that I developed early on was the skill of repetition. On a consistent and continual basis, I constantly recite poetry, inspirational quotations, interesting facts and figures, and other tidbits of information that help to shape a well-rounded repertoire. To some, this may seem to be a bit odd, particularly if they were to pass my shower stall at 6:00 A.M., only to find me deep in throes of a good Robert Frost poem. But I have found that this, believe it or not, is the best means at my disposal for keeping myself sharp and staying at the top of my game.

> *Two roads diverged in a yellow wood,*
> *And sorry I could not travel both*
> *And be one traveler, long I stood*
> *And looked down one as far as I could*
> *To where it bent in the undergrowth;...* [9]

Today, as The Architect of Change™, "America's leading advocate for achieving greatness by embracing change," I have discovered the importance of practicing to stay prepared. As a result of this continuous training, I have had the privilege of addressing groups as small as ten and as large as 10,000, having now become an expert at relating to others through the powerful medium of communication.

Growing up as a child, I often heard the phrase, "Please be patient with me. God is not through with me yet." Understanding that as a fallible human being there is truth enshrined in this simple saying, I have come to accept the fact that I will mess up most of the time. But in doing so, I must always remember, "When you mess up, look up. Nothing beats a failure but a try." If that be the case, then I am well on my way toward a life of never-ending self-improvement. In Japanese business culture, for example, there is a unique concept known as *kaizen*, which is literally defined as "continuous improvement." It is often used by those who are responsible for the development of products upon which they constantly improve, such as Nissan and Honda automobiles. In fact, in the Japanese world of kaizen, nothing is ever really finished to a state of final completion, as everything done can be improved upon.

As you strive for a license to live your dreams, understanding that everyone comes with baggage and dings in their exterior, ask yourself: "What are some of the things that I can improve upon starting today?" Not tomorrow. Not next week. Right now! Are there relationships I would like to improve—*right now?* Are there mistakes I would like to correct—*right now?* Am I practicing *kaizen?* Am I "continuously improving?"

 ### Rearview Glance: "Lights, Camera, Action"

On a cool December morning in Los Angeles, California, the 4th to be exact, I sat in an audience with the inimitable Les Brown, inspirational speaker extraordinaire. He was hosting a "Discover Your Power Voice" training program in which I was privileged to participate. During this training Les and Dr. Julie Van Putten, a medical supervisor and speaker-trainer, taught us the nuances of speaking to an audience in a way that captivates the mind and compels the individual to step into your story. At this time I was alerted to a pleasant surprise. "Young man," Les Brown said to me as I listened with great intent, "tonight we are going to have some cameras here and they will be taping for a possible show. And I want you to get up and do your thing." Humbled, I obliged and began putting together a speech in my mind. "You'll have two minutes, maybe three." "I'll take four minutes, maybe five," I joked. It took nine minutes, maybe ten. But the audience loved it and I was grateful. My point in all of this, as Les taught us that weekend (that we should "never tell a story without it having a point, and you should never make a point without having a story"), was the fact that I was prepared when called upon and ready to "do my thing."

## Universal Road Rule: "Use It or Lose It"

As a child growing up in the Christian tradition, I was often taught that my gifts and talents should be used to the glory of the Creator and the benefit of all humankind. Whether in a large public setting or a small private one, using those gifts is essential to maintaining the presence of that gift itself. Much worse, to not use that gift was a form of personal heresy and a squandering of what was within me that could have benefitted the world. For example, in the medical sense, not using a muscle is known as muscular atrophy, often resulting in the decrease in size and wasting of muscle tissue. Muscles that lose their nerve supply can atrophy and simply waste away. The same applies to the gifts that lie within you, given to you as a tool at birth and only diminished by your lack of care and nurturing. "Use it or lose it" applies to each of us and must be the inspiration for continued improvement. But what exactly should you "use or lose" as you travel along your way?

## Real Life Road Map: "Time, Talent, and Treasure"

"Service is the price you pay for your space here on earth." As trustees of an inheritance greater than we deserve, I believe that everyone is required to give back a portion of who we are and what we have to help make the world a better place. Whether it means spending one hour a week mentoring a young person; using your special skills, talents, and qualifications for the good of humankind; or giving a percentage of your earnings to help uplift the lives of the "least of these," the Universe requires us to give something back. Now, I am not saying that you should be as gullible as Gomer Pyle, but use your discretion in giving—and give anyway! Perform due diligence and, after all references have been checked, give to the best of your ability of the three things that everyone has, and some in ample supply: time, talent, and treasure.

## Give of Your Time

The iconic American business leader, Lee Iacocca, once declared, "The thing that lies at the foundation of positive change, the way I see it, is service to a fellow human being."[10] Research conducted by the Corporation for National and Community Service recently found that people who volunteer live longer than those who do not. Data also shows that volunteering increases levels of life satisfaction, self-esteem, and happiness and that people who volunteer often see tangible benefits (to body and soul) by "donating" just 40-100 hours per year of their time. The great motivational speaker, Jim Rohn, once said, "Time is more valuable than money. You can get more money, but you cannot get more time."[11] With the time that you have been given here on earth, what are you doing? How are you spending it? How willing have you been to give your time to worthy causes that benefit society as a whole? As a conscientious traveler along the highways of life, it is important to remember that giving to others is a fundamental part of the rules of the road.

## Give of Your Talent

As a child growing up, my mother often told me that talent and 50 cents might get me a cup of coffee. Famed Basketball great, John

Wooden once said, "Talent is God-given. Be humble. Fame is man-given. Be grateful. Conceit is self-given. Be careful."[12] Have you always been a safe driver? And, if you haven't been safe, have you been careful? As you take an honest inventory of your character within, are you using the talents and skills that the Good Master gave you for the uplifting of humankind?

## Give of Your Treasure

Henry David Thoreau once said, "If you give money, spend yourself with it." Everyone in the world has something to give. Whether you are a prince or you are a pauper, all people have something that is of significant value to themselves in their possession or immediate control. With that being said, I also believe that it is required of all of us to give a portion of the things we place value on to the benefit of others. Whether it means paying your taxes, paying your tithes, or giving to your favorite civic or nonprofit charity, it is important to give to the benefit of the less-fortunate members of our society. As a licensed operator on the turnpikes of time, think of it as an occasional toll that you must pay as you move from point to point. And when you give, give of all that you have—in the right spirit and intent—don't do it because of. Do it in spite of. Do it anyway!

> People are often unreasonable, illogical, and self-centered; Forgive them anyway. If you are kind, people may accuse you of selfish, ulterior motives; Be kind anyway. If you are successful, you will win some false friends and some true enemies; Succeed anyway. If you are honest and frank, people may cheat you; Be honest and frank anyway. What you spend years building,

someone could destroy overnight; Build anyway. If you find serenity and happiness, they may be jealous; Be happy anyway. The good you do today, people will often forget tomorrow; Do good anyway. Give the world the best you have and it may just never be enough; Give the world the best you have anyway. You see, in the final analysis, it's all between you and God; It was never between you and them anyway.[13] —Mother Teresa

 ### Red Light Challenge: "Pass With Flying Colors"

Throughout modern history, the best means by which communities, organizations, companies, and governments have used to measure an individual's aptitude have been tests. Famed American writer Richard Bach observed, "Here is the test to find whether your mission on earth is finished. If you're alive, it isn't."[14] As long as you live, you will be faced with tests of some sort. Whether they're tests in school or tests in life, passing with flying colors ought to be your objective when called to the task. As such, passing a road test before getting our operational permit is the first and most fundamental prerequisite we must meet before we are granted a license to proceed safely down the highways and byways of life. Just as importantly, testing before licensing is generally the most efficient method used to ensure that we are not a danger to ourselves or to others when we get behind the wheel. Life itself is quite similar in that we will be tested with trials and tribulations from time to time, and how we respond will have an immediate effect on how we will be graded in the end.

## Roadside Response: "The Test of a Man"

As mentioned in the Introduction, growing up in sunny South Florida was like living in what Charles Dickens would have called *A Tale of Two Cities:*

> It was the best of times, it was the worst of times; it was the age of wisdom, it was the age of foolishness; it was the epoch of belief, it was the epoch of incredulity; it was the season of Light, it was the season of Darkness; it was the spring of hope, it was the winter of despair; we had everything before us, we had nothing before us; we were all going directly to Heaven, we were all going the other way.[15]

Palm Beach County, Florida, where I was born and raised, boasts some of the wealthiest areas in all of America. Worth Avenue and the Breakers Hotel in Palm Beach are just a stone's throw away from the dilapidated area I lived in called, of all things, "Pleasant City." An overrun and rundown part of West Palm Beach, cut off by a dividing wall down the middle that separated the poor from the rich, Pleasant City was a "planned community." With streets called "Happy" and "Joyful," it was called home by the socio-economically disadvantaged people of Palm Beach County, usually poor blacks, Hispanics, and woefully down-on-their-luck whites. The first test that I had to pass was keeping an indomitable determination to succeed and excel despite my beginnings and growing up with a lack of resources.

As an initiate into Alpha Phi Alpha, I memorized a poem nearly twenty years ago, "The Test of a Man," that continues to help guide my actions today:

*The test of a man is the fight that he makes; the grit that he daily shows.*
*The way that he stands upon his feet and takes life's numerous bumps and blows.*

*A coward can smile when there's naught to fear and nothing his progress bars.*
*But it takes a man to stand a cheer when the other fellow stars.*

*It isn't the victory after all, but the fight that a fellow makes.*
*A man, when driven against the wall still stands erect.*
*And takes the blows of fate with his head held high;*
*Bleeding and bruised and pale is the man who will win,*
*And fate defied, for he isn't afraid to fail.*

Before you can pass any test with flying colors, whether it be a driving test or the "test of a man," one's willingness to "lose and start again at your beginnings," as Rudyard Kipling once implored, is a critical component of eventual success.

My purpose from early on in life has been some form of public service. For me, that began in the fourth grade in my first run for office as class president. There, in grade school, having been bitten by the bug of service, I found myself passing the test of *service above self* as a passionate way of life. I believe this was a great equalizer that allowed me to compete and win against those with seemingly infinite resources, by sheer strength of personality, influence, and an ability to produce. Since my days in Pleasant City, I have gone on to meet four presidents of the United States, to work in the halls of the United States Capitol and on Wall Street, and to travel the world extensively, spreading hope and possibility to the "least of these," while never forgetting from whence I came. Even still, however, I was tested at every turn in ways that have helped me to develop a true license to live in spite of overwhelming obstacles.

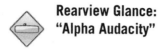

### Rearview Glance: "Alpha Audacity"

Author Marianne Williamson so poignantly observed:

Our deepest fear is not that we are inadequate. Our deepest fear is that we are powerful beyond measure. It is our light, not our darkness, that most frightens us. We ask ourselves, who am I to be brilliant, gorgeous, talented, and fabulous? Actually, who are you not to be? You are a child of God. Your playing small doesn't serve the world. There's nothing enlightened about shrinking so that other people won't feel insecure around you. We are all meant to shine, as children do. We are born to make manifest the glory of God that is within us. It's not just in some of us, it's in everyone. And as we let our own light shine, we unconsciously give other people permission to do the same. As we are liberated from our own fear, our presence automatically liberates others.[16]

At the age of 33 I had, to some, the unmitigated gall, the "audacity" even, to launch a quixotic campaign to become the youngest national president in the oldest black fraternity in America. Boasting of such members as eight sitting United States Congressmen, several sitting mayors, the late Rev. Dr. Martin Luther King Jr., and Supreme Court Justice Thurgood Marshall, Alpha Phi Alpha Fraternity, Inc. had just crossed a centennial threshold and an election was on for a new leader. Having been intimately involved in the operational machinations of the organization, having served on its international board of directors, as Chief of Staff to a former national president, and an employee of its corporate headquarters, I believed I knew the fraternity and what it wanted for a new millennium. What I hadn't taken into account, however, was my own hubris and arrogance at thinking that I was prepared for such an awesome task of leadership—at that time—that would ultimately be my electoral undoing.

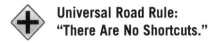

## Universal Road Rule: "There Are No Shortcuts."

Beautiful Italian film actress Sophia Loren once said: "Mistakes are the dues we pay for a full life."[17] As a young Turk destined to change the world and the way it did business, I learned—early on—that there was no getting past making mistakes and, just as importantly, there is no getting past paying your dues either. Whether you are starting out in life or in your driving career, there will come inevitable tolls in the road that slow down your progress and require you to contribute a bit of what you have in order to get to where you are going. Recognizing that it is better to be a patron than a scofflaw is an important step that one must take before pulling out of the driveway.

Brian Klemmer reminds us in his book *If How-To's Were Enough, We Would All Be Skinny, Rich and Happy* that life is about taking the proverbial bull by the horns and controlling your own destiny. To that end, one of the greatest lessons I have ever learned in life was the immutable fact that life isn't fair—and it's not equitable—get over it! Moreover, we must also remember that there are no quick solutions to fast success. There is no magic bullet and, chances are, you won't win the lottery. So...what are you going to do about it? In fact, I would venture to say that any overnight success was years in the making. No one is going to give you anything in life (and if they do, it won't last very long). With that thought in mind, it is important to remember that there are no shortcuts on the path to success. As such, you must be willing to "run the race that is set before you," enduring the ups and the downs that will come with life's ultimate failures and successes (see Heb. 12:1). Just as importantly, one must never forget that paying your dues is a fundamental prerequisite for getting to where you want to go. Attempting to take a detour around this unavoidable toll road is nothing more than an exercise in futility that will only frustrate you and leave you back where you started from. Get over it by going through it—savoring every step, every yard, every mile of the way.

 ### Real Life Road Map: "Read Signs Carefully"

Stress, we know, is a silent killer that slowly saps the lifeblood out of us, until it ultimately takes our life one way or another because of our failure to manage it properly. As classic overachievers, oftentimes people like myself tend to misread or simply ignore signs we pass along the side of the road. Sometimes these are warning signs and at others they are merely directional, but not paying attention to them—or, even worse, pretending they don't exist—is a surefire way to an unmitigated disaster and possibly to an early grave. Knowing the signs to look for is the first and most fundamental prerequisite of any licensed driver. Some signs give us a heads up; maybe there is traffic or a detour that can save us some time. Moreover, ignoring signs is not an option, as doing so is a great risk to the driver and costly for society. You can't go 80 mph in a 25-mph zone for very long.

Our bodies are a lot like our cars. The problem is, many of us treat our cars a lot better than we do our own bodies. Cars are replaceable but our bodies are not. Many of us still choose to ignore the signs of stress, which is exactly how and why this silent killer is so prevalent in our society. The following are some of the signs and physical effects that stress can have on your body, which, if ignored, can negatively affect your capacity to positively change the world one community at a time. You need to make sure you stay healthy so you can carry the torch for future generations:

- Facial tension (tight lips, clenched jaw, etc.)

- Tongue clicking or teeth grinding

- Dark circles under eyes

- Facial sweating (on forehead or upper lip)

- High blood pressure

- Heart disease (For 50% of men and 63% of women, the first symptom of heart disease is death. Many don't have a chance to have a second heart attack because the first one killed them.)

- Overweight (less than 20% based on your Body Mass Index) or obese (20% or more).

If you or someone you know, love, or care about exhibits these "symptoms" of oxidative stress, I encourage you to remember the old saying, "An ounce of prevention is worth a pound of cure."

Let me ask you a question: If you happened to be driving down the road in your new car and the oil light all of a sudden started to flash, would you put a Band-Aid over the light and keep driving? No, you would probably pull over and check the oil and add some if need be.

The light is the symptom, but the oil shortage is the cause. However, physically, many of us use Band-Aids or take drugs to cover up the symptoms instead of fixing the root cause of the problem.

What would happen if we forgot that the truck we are driving runs on diesel fuel, not the unleaded gasoline we just filled the tank with? The truck would probably not go very far because it was not designed to be driven with that type of fuel. If you decided to continue driving it, the gasoline would cause damage to the engine and eventually break the truck, and it would cost quite a lot to fix.

Our bodies work in much the same way. We were designed to consume specific "fuel"—nutrition. The refined, denatured, processed, green harvested, genetically modified, irradiated, factory food most of us consume from time to time when we are in a rush is not the proper "fuel" needed to maintain our wellness and vitality. If you went out running one day and you started to get thirsty, you wouldn't go down to the doctor's office and ask for a drug to treat the "symptoms" of thirst, your dry throat, and lack of energy. And you wouldn't go to the naturopath for an herbal remedy or the chiropractor for an adjustment—you would fix the "cause" of your thirst by drinking a glass of water.

Taking one drug to treat the symptoms of arthritis or another drug to treat the symptoms of allergies makes about as much sense as taking a drug to treat the symptoms of thirst. This is true especially when, on average, 106,000 people die and 2.2 million are harmed each year because of adverse reactions to properly prescribed prescription drugs in a hospital setting, making it the number 4 leading cause of death in America![18] Many agree that it's much easier and a lot less expensive to fix the root cause of the problem rather than playing "Russian Roulette" trying to manage the symptoms with pharmaceutical drugs.

These deadly, debilitating, destructive, addictive, toxic prescription drugs now kill three times as many people per year as heroin, cocaine, marijuana, and all methamphetamines combined! Only heart disease, cancer, and strokes kill more Americans than drugs prescribed by doctors. In medical parlance, this is known as *iatrogenocide*.

Now, I'm not saying that drugs don't have their place. Shoot, if I tear up my knee running and have to get surgery, you better believe I want to be knocked out cold for that procedure! America is great at trauma care. If I had to get in a car accident, I would not want to have it happen anywhere else. However, according to the World Health Organization, the United States is now in 72nd place for chronic illness and disease even though we spend more on medical care than any other country. You would be shocked to find out what countries we are trailing.

Something is very, very wrong. The focus needs to be on wellness and prevention rather than the "free sickness" paradigm. We all remember growing up learning about cavities and tooth decay, which are mainly caused by not brushing or flossing our teeth. My dentist always told me to "only floss the teeth you want to keep." Most of us heeded that advice and do it daily to prevent cavities. However, most of the folks in our society are still not actively doing much to prevent the oxidative stress and premature aging that is taking place because of the highly stressful and toxic environment many of us find ourselves living in.

In the last 30 years we have been told that there are 84 new autoimmune disorders and 30 new forms of cancer. However, if we think about it for a second, we realize that the root cause of, let's say, cancer is *not* because of a chemotherapy deficiency. It's not like my mom gave me a bunch of chemo in my bottle as a baby and you didn't get any, and that's why you have cancer and I don't.

Thirty years ago, when we had black and white televisions, eight-tracks, and typewriters, the standard of care for cancer was chemotherapy, radiation, and surgery. Thirty years later, we have digital cameras, DVDs, and MP3s—you can even watch television on your cell phone—yet the standard of care for cancer is still chemo, radiation, and surgery. To me, that smells a little fishy. Despite the billions that have been spent over the decades, cancer has gone from the number 8 killer in America to number 2, killing someone every minute of every day. The treatment of cancer is now a trillion-dollar-a-year business. People's lives, incomes, and careers depend on other people getting cancer. Could that be a reason we are not seeing much improvement in chronic illness and disease? Could there be too much money at stake, too many jobs on the line "treating symptoms" instead of fixing the root cause?

We all know that our bodies are made up of trillions of cells. You see, healthy cells make up healthy tissues, which in turn make up healthy organs. Healthy organs make up healthy systems, which in turn make up a healthy body. That's easy to remember.

In fact, one could argue that there really is only one "disease," the root cause being the malfunction and breakdown of our cells. If the cells in the joints are malfunctioning and breaking down, it's called "arthritis." If it happens in the colon it's called "colitis." If the cells are malfunctioning and breaking down in the pancreas, we call that "diabetes." In the brain it could be Alzheimer's or Parkinson's, but it is all really the same thing. The cells are all jacked up. It's practically impossible for your cells to be healthy yet for you to be sick.

So, what we need to focus on is the balancing of our cells. Scientists have discovered, with those super microscopes that can read DNA and map the human genome, that our cells have five functions that are needed to stay healthy. Our cells need to be fed, cleansed, regulated, defended/repaired, and, most importantly, they must communicate correctly with each other. Picture yourself putting new tires on your car. The most important thing to remember for a smooth, safe, and comfortable ride is that you need to make sure that each of the tires has to have the same amount of air in them. Imagine trying to drive down the highway at 65 MPH with only two of your tires filled with air. It would be a pretty bumpy ride!

Well, each function of the cell is like a tire on your car. When we balance each of them in our bodies, we have a healthy and smooth ride as well! People have asked me, "Elvin, what are the most important nutrients?" I would suggest that the most important nutrients are the ones that we are missing.

You see, there are some essentials that we must have to survive. We must have:

- Fresh air (We can't go very long without oxygen.)

- Clean, fluoride-free, purified, alkaline water (We can only go a couple days without $H_2O$.)

- 8 essential amino acids

- 2 essential fatty acids

- 72 trace minerals

- 26 essential vitamins (They are called *essential* because if you are missing any one of them, you could die. As an example, let's say we decided to take away Vitamin C from our diets. Well, we would eventually come down with a "disease" called scurvy which, as many sailors discovered 400 years ago, could and did kill them if they didn't add limes and oranges to their diets. You can take someone all the way up to their deathbed with scurvy and at the last moment, feed them vitamin C and their scurvy will go away. In short, scurvy is simply a Vitamin C deficiency.)

- 8 essential glyconutrients needed for proper cellular communication (A quick read of Chapter 56 in the *Harpers Biochemistry Medical Text* lists them all. Unfortunately, in our diets today we are only getting two of the eight monosaccharides needed to make glycoprotein on the ends of our cells. We are missing six! Fortunately, savvy scientists have already discovered, named, created, and patented a new technology that has the combination of all eight of these sugars in one product.)

The study of essential sugars is the newest and most exciting—and controversial—field of research in medicine right now. In 2003, MIT's technology review journal called glycomics, the study of these essential sugars, one of the top ten technologies that will change the world. *Science Magazine*, *Scientific American*, and countless other peer review journals called the study of these sugars and how they affect our body's ability to heal and repair itself "medicine's last frontier." Nobel Prizes in medicine have even been awarded to scientists researching this new and exciting field of research.

My family and I daily take and freely recommend an incredible wellness system that helps to balance each of the five functions of the cells. I highly encourage you to do some research on these incredibly important, missing nutrients that are no longer found in our diets. Start taking them and sharing them with friends and loved ones who want to stay healthy and energetic for as long as possible!

The world needs you and the gifts within you that only you can share. My goal is to do my part to help keep you alive and well as long as possible for you to manifest your destiny.

Chapter 4

# GET YOUR MOTOR RUNNING

AFTER YOU have gone through the process of study and examination, with the ultimate conferring of a driver's license to signal to others that you meet the basic requirements for operating a motor vehicle, the time has finally come for you to "get your motor running and head out on the highway." So too, upon embarking on a journey of self-discovery and actualization in life, putting "rubber to the road" is the only way any of us can achieve any measure of success. To that end, it is imperative to remember, as a newly minted sojourner down the streets of future success, that you begin with the end in mind. Understand that if you don't know where you are going, any road will take you there.

For nearly 45 years, the world has driven a little easier, with very little fanfare or recognition for those who have helped to make their travels from one place to the next more efficient. Established in 1967 as the Cartographic Services Division of R.R. Donnelly & Sons in Chicago, the venerable travel staple has helped to point billions of travelers in the right direction as they went their ways. That company would eventually come to be known as MapQuest. Today, having become the most visited map Website on the Internet, MapQuest guides more than 40 million users monthly, reducing frustration and confusion for drivers in unfamiliar territory and those with whom they share the roadways.

As conscientious travelers concerned about truly maximizing the unknown amount of time we are given to get to our life's destinations, having a clear road map that takes into account roadblocks, detours, and other potential obstacles is critical. A good map not only helps us arrive on time to our ultimate destination, but it helps us to arrive at all. After the path has been plotted, however, it is then incumbent upon the person behind the wheel to proceed with caution. As you enter traffic, keep your eyes wide open and an ear to the ground, looking for anything that could potentially stifle your progress or cause a breakdown.

## Check Your Surroundings

An ancient African proverb states, "No man tests the depths of the water with both feet." Having passed all the appropriate tests required of a licensed life operator, it is important to remember that you check out your surroundings before you put your keys in the ignition and shift your vehicle into gear. Moreover, as you assume all the rights and privileges appertaining thereto, it is important when getting started to first observe your surroundings. Take a complete safety inspection around your vehicle before you ever start adjusting the mirrors. Life is quite similar in that it is critical that you clear out any obvious obstructions that stand between you and your destination. In doing so, you are better able to clear an unobstructed path to success at every level.

Noted English biologist Thomas Henry Huxley once reminded us, "A well-worn adage advises those who set out upon a great enterprise to count the cost."[1] As you strive to successfully maneuver to a position that will allow you to more easily reach your objectives in life, remember that the caution light is a part of the traffic sequence for a reason! A great example of this can be found in the world of carpentry, where the first and most important rule that both the apprentice and seasoned master must abide by is simple in concept but critical for success: *"Measure twice. Cut once."* In short, always remember to count the costs before making any decisions that you may ultimately live to regret.

Another important carpentry lesson that has particular resonance for those who strive to compete and win in the game of life is to always—*always*—pay very close attention to detail. Carpentry is one of the world's oldest and most exact professions. According to Jereme Green, an expert carpenter and skilled tradesman versed in the importance of "checking your surroundings," the basic rule is to always be mindful of the little things that may seem innocuous at first glance. If left unattended, these little things can throw a serious monkey wrench in your plans for project completion.

> There are so many things that can be looked over or forgotten on a carpentry job, such as running out of material or out of supplies. Train your mind and eyes to look for details and be observant and aware of your surroundings.[2]

 ### Red Light Challenge: "Take an Honest Inventory"

Perhaps one of the toughest things to do as a human being is to be honest with ourselves through the process of self-inventory and discovery. As French theologian, poet, and writer Francois Fenelon said, "Nothing will make us so charitable and tender to the faults of others, as, by self-examination, thoroughly to know our own."[3]

As a Professional Life, Career, and Corporate Coach on track to become a Certified Master Coach with the International Coach Federation, I was taught the importance of understanding oneself before truly beginning to understand others. This means asking the right questions that help to clarify and enlighten just who we are and what we are made of. In her article, "Expert Question Asking: The Engine of Successful Coaching," Dr. Marilee C. Goldberg observes:

> Questions are fundamental for gathering information; building and maintaining relationships; learning; thinking clearly, creatively and critically; making requests; and initiating action. Asking questions is also fundamental for resolving conflicts and breakdowns, making decisions, solving problems, instigating out of the box thinking, listening fully and maintaining individual and organizational change.[4]

Today I use those skills to help bridge the gap within my own life between where I am and where I want to be. I have found that the only way in which I can truly step into my greatness is with a simple acknowledgment of who I am and what makes me tick. This, of course, begins with the leaven of self-examination.

In his editorial aptly named "The Examined Life," author Harry C. Meserve intoned:

> We know less about ourselves than any other portion of society, and our lack of self-knowledge is now our most antisocial problem...Today, as in the Athens Socrates knew, most of us live unexamined lives, or at best, lives so superficially understood that we are aware only of a nameless anxiety that whispers the disconcerting message that there is so much more to

know about the sources, the motives, the meaning about what we say and do.[5]

As individuals who only get one chance to live this life, we must do so with gusto, panache, and an understanding that true life springs from within. As such, it is critically important that we regularly exam the condition of our own lives, particularly where we stand in relation to others, especially those we love, so that we truly get the most out of this all-too-brief journey we take during our time here on earth.

## Roadside Response: "Know Thyself!"

The ancient Egyptians, when erecting temples of worship throughout the African landscape, inscribed a thought-provoking message above the doorposts of every public facility. "Know Thyself," the inscription read, serving as a continual, visible reminder for those who read it to ask themselves the right questions as they searched for the right answers for themselves and their lives. As an eighteen-year-old freshman student at Hampton University in Hampton, Virginia, I desperately wanted to belong. Having served as class president nearly every year since the fourth grade, I think it was safe to say that my desire to serve, coupled with my need for acceptance, was strong enough to guide me to make, what turned out for me, to be a series of crucial decisions that would guide my steps for many years to come. Many of those decisions included, among other things, my choice of a college that I believed would help me to grow and become a better person, while learning more about myself, my culture, and the history of my own people, three things that are critically important when it comes to truly knowing yourself. At that time, my world centered on joining and becoming deeply enmeshed in the inner sanctum of the world's oldest Black Fraternity, Alpha Phi Alpha, a group of distinguished gentlemen with which I wanted to affiliate. What I did not quite realize at the time, however, was that this journey of acceptance by others would quickly become a key turning point in my quest toward self-actualization.

As a student at a relatively conservative and traditional historically black college, there were a series of qualifications that I had to "pass" before I was allowed the opportunity to seek admission into a fraternity. One of those caveats was to have a "zero balance" with the university, meaning I had to have no monies owed to the university at the time of my induction or I would not be allowed to proceed with the initiation process. For me, as a scholarship cadet in the Army ROTC program, I had to make an immediate choice upon returning to school the second semester of my sophomore year, the point at which I was academically eligible to join the fraternity, and that choice was to either stay on campus and render myself ineligible to pledge that semester (as staying on campus would have meant I owed a debt of room and board to the university and, as such, would be ineligible for initiation), or take a risk and become homeless that semester, in order to achieve my dreams. For me, the choice was easy. I decided to take my chances braving the elements and depending upon the generosity of others before I would allow this coveted opportunity to pass me by. For many, this would appear to be borderline insane, as no one voluntarily chooses homelessness as a means of advancing ahead. For me, however, this was something that had to be done if I wanted to achieve the ultimate goal of self-awareness and camaraderie that I so desperately needed at that vulnerable and formative stage of my life.

Throughout my "semester abroad" as I refer to it now, I slept on other people's couches, floors, and wherever I could during that harsh and challenging spring, so that I could become a member of the "Black & Old Gold," as the Alphas often referred to themselves. What I learned from this experience, however, is a better understanding of myself and the things that were important to me. In fact, during that timeframe, I learned the old adage, "successful people are willing to do the things today that others won't do, to have the things tomorrow that others won't have." Just as importantly, I learned what it means to be completely dependent upon the grace of God and the generosity of others who would help me through this trying time in my life. Fortunately for me, and to the dismay of my genuinely concerned mother, I completed my grueling admissions process into the organization, but not before I learned more about myself and my ability to endure just about anything, if I was willing to hunker down, ride out the storm, and never give up on my dreams. Today, I am proud to say that joining the fraternity was one of the most important decisions I ever made, providing me not only with a built-in infrastructure of brothers and friends who are willing to support me when I need them. More importantly, however, it taught me things I never knew about myself that helps to rule my heart, guide my thoughts and control my mind so that, through Him, I may continue to be "a servant of all."

### Rearview Glance: "Go With Your Gut"

As a firm believer in spiritual gifts given to us at the time of our birth, as well as those that we acquire I have been fortunate in that I have been granted many gifts and talents that have served me well as I travel along my way. For as long as I can remember, one of the greatest tools in my toolbox of life is the gift known to many as discernment—the ability to rather quickly assess individuals whom I come into contact with, to determine if they are friend or foe. On more than one occasion, I have been the fortunate beneficiary of this amazing gift, having been confronted with supporters and scoundrels alike and having to distinguish between the two. Often I found this most beneficial when reviewing and assessing potential employees and team members as leaders or titular heads of various departments, groups, and organizations.

One of the most difficult times I have ever had in the work world came at the hands of a very bitter and sad individual, often referred to by her employees as "The Dragon Lady." Apparently, she believed that her purpose in life was to spread her misery into the lives of others—whether they liked it or not. Knowing that I had an ability to read situations and people—even though he didn't quite know what the gift itself was called—my supervisor soon looked to me to provide sound advice and counsel on how he should proceed with this most crucial hire. "I wouldn't hire this person if I were you," I recall saying. I had listened to a "gut feeling" that revealed to me the amount of pain and pressure behind the smile that those who experienced this woman's wrath would ultimately have to endure. My supervisor, however, summarily overruled my objections and pressed on anyway.

Not less than two weeks after showing the workplace her well-behaved representative, *"Madam Dragonista"* began to rear her ugly head. From that point until the time she would leave our place of employment in a blaze of guts and glory, she proceeded to single-handedly harass and harangue her subordinates with unreasonable requests and berating comments. She even had an uncanny knack for making grown men cry with her exceptionally mean-spirited nature. One day, completely exasperated by the sheer anguish that I was being subjected to under the auspices of this petite "people-eater," I finally reached my breaking point. Something had to give.

"Sir," I told the big boss, "I just can't take it anymore. This devil-spawn you hired (against my suggestion, I might add), has gotten on the pits of my last nerve! I refuse to be mistreated by her any further."

"Hang in there," he admonished me. "Tell her how you feel!"

As I sat and listened, I couldn't believe my ears. "With all due respect, sir, I have decided that today is the last day I am putting up with her crap. She has dogged me out for the last time and, if it is the last thing I do, I intend to let her know exactly how I feel."

"Well, surely there must be some sort of redeeming value to the relationship?" he asked, as I sat, at this point, on the brink of tears.

"Well, actually, sir, the only positive benefit I have received from working with her is a closer relationship with God."

"Why, what do you mean?" he inquired, to which I informed him that, having endured the bulk of her mistreatment for weeks and months on end, I had come to develop a closer relationship with the Almighty Creator as a result of reporting to her.

"I am fasting and praying that I don't kill this woman!" I screamed, "You have got to do something about this!"

Unfortunately this would continue for another 18 months. In fact, it wasn't until she embarked upon a journey to enact an office-style coup to take him out that the boss finally did something about it. Quietly, over a holiday break, when the office was closed for several weeks, he moved to help her "transition into other employment opportunities," hoping to never hear from this morale-destroying individual again.

"Why do you think she acted that way?" my boss asked me one day. "To be honest with you, sir, it's because you let her," I replied. You must never forget that, as the leader, the buck stops with you!

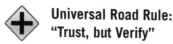

## Universal Road Rule: "Trust, but Verify"

Having been born in the early 1970s, I came of age during the era of the Reagan Revolution. It was a time when the United States was embroiled in an expanding Cold War arms race with the Soviet Union. The political landscape, while fractured, was one in which individuals were given the benefit of the doubt—to a certain extent— when it came to taking the word of others (particularly those who were diametrically or politically opposed to the positions their antagonists espoused). During this time when peaceful, sovereign nations were being invaded and overrun by military aggressors, a phrase was repeatedly used by President Reagan to reiterate his willingness to believe his enemies (to a certain extent), so long as what they were saying could be reinforced with cold, hard facts.

In 1987, at the signing of the Intermediate Range Nuclear Forces (INF) Treaty, President Reagan was addressing the proposals proffered by his Soviet counterpart, Mikhail Gorbachev. Reagan used a well-worn Soviet proverb that came to exemplify his wariness about the growing relationship between the two woefully estranged superpowers. *"Doveryai, no proveryai,"* Reagan declared at the signing of the historic arms reduction treaty. *"Trust, but verify."* Having heard it on more than one occasion from the president of the United States, the Soviet leader responded flatly and rather coolly, "You repeat that at every meeting." To which President Reagan responded in a classic rejoinder, "I like it!"

As you strive to live the life that you deserve and are destined to achieve—if you only just believe—it is important to remember that you should always aim to verify the soundness and safety of any course you are about to travel. First, check your surroundings for any avoidable obstructions and delays to your progress. Then, verify that all "i's" have been dotted and "t's" have been crossed before you embark upon your journey. Just like Ronald Reagan did so many years ago, have faith in those who stand before you making claims that may (or may not) have an immediate impact upon the journey that you are on. With faith, however, comes a bit of common sense, understanding that you should be *"wise as serpents, and harmless as doves"* when dealing with any unknown situation or new course of action (see Matt. 10:16). After all, "Fool me once shame on you—fool me twice shame on me."

## Real Life Road Map: "METT-T Dependent"

"Failing to plan is planning to fail," it has often been said. Having worked as a logistician responsible for people, freight, and time-lines, and having been trained in military protocols and procedures as a Reserve Officers Training Corp Cadet for the United States Army, I understand the importance of planning all the way to the end. Making sure that I have an action plan (and several backup plans) is critical to achieving my goal. At the point where you are in your life right now, whether at the beginning of your journey, well into the flow of traffic, or having exited the highway and cooled your heels at a rest stop, having a plan on how to get to where you want to go is the first and most important step.

As a young and rebellious cadet in Hampton University's Pirate Battalion, I didn't learn much of what I needed to while sitting in my military science courses. But one concept I did learn was repeated to me over and over again: the concept that most things are dependent upon a set of constantly changing variables that we must learn to hurdle and overcome if we are to ever achieve our objective. In military parlance, this is known by the acronym METT-T (pronounced Met-TEE) and, as I would soon learn, almost everything was dependent upon that. I soon found out that the military has its own language that actually means something, when spoken in correct sequence, to the millions of valiant men and women who serve and have served in uniform for the protection of their nation. If you don't believe that, try this on for size:

> As a student cadet, I often had to wake up every morning, three to five days a week, to go to PT at 0500 hours. Upon arrival, after we fell in for roll call, my BC would ask my PL for a SITREP, who would then turn to the LT who would, in turn, lean on the MSGT for the numbers and the count. Afterward, we would perform a vigorous PT session, followed by 18-minute drills and hip pocket training that would get us ready for such things as the BRM that we would cover on the PTX the coming weekend. And all I would get was an MRE and KP duties for my troubles!

Which takes us to METT-T...Still with me?

METT-T is a military acronym for the following: "Mission, Enemy, Time, Terrain—Troops," and serves as code for "anything you want to do is always dependent on something else." And, chances are, more often than not, it is completely out of your purview or your ability to control. What you can control, however, is your ability to respond in a way that is meaningful and prudent to whatever situation you are confronted with.

As a driver along the highways of life, you must always remember to be prepared for anything: buckle up and drive carefully! It really is a jungle out there!

## Mission

What is your mission in life and are you doing what needs to be done to fulfill it? If not, why not? If you don't know what your mission, purpose, or passion is, have you begun to ask yourself the right questions? *"If not you. . .then who? If not now. . .then when?"*

## Enemy

*"In life, friends come and go but enemies accumulate."* As you proceed with caution down the highways and the side streets, always keep in mind that there are enemies out there—some real and some imagined—and your job is to distinguish which ones pose a clear and present danger to your ability to live a life of freedom and abundance. Perhaps your greatest enemy is closer than you think. *"We have seen the enemy and the enemy is us."*

## Time

The journey of discovery you undertake in this world is finite. Even the "License to Live" we often take for granted will come eventually to the point of expiration. Therefore, valuing time and the fact that it too is limited is important to your life's journey. Do a diagnostic check on how you spend your time and be willing to adjust your speed in certain areas if you are teetering on the edge of reckless endangerment.

## Terrain

Before beginning any journey, it is important that you get to know the lay of the land and have a basic understanding of topography— whether it be geographic, political, a combination of the two, or something else completely. Understanding terrain is critical to traveling a route via the path of least resistance. Without the time-saving skill of knowing how to read a map, you are almost destined for failure—you may very well end up in a valley full of quicksand simply because you couldn't tell a mountain from a molehill.

## Troops

As you aim to steer yourself and your future into the right direction, understand that you will not arrive at any place of real significance in this life without the help of someone else. Protecting your troops, the people on your team, who would regularly go to bat for you or— better yet, take a bullet for you—is something that must be mastered by an individual duly licensed to live a life of great expectations. Moreover, having empathy for those around you who work hard every day to uplift the lives of the "least of these" through the strength of their labor and the power of their example, is critical to your own success. Knowing your troops and being sensitive to their needs will, in turn, enable you to receive the support and continued "followership" of those who will respond to your call in the hour of need.

Chapter 5

# OBJECTS IN MIRROR
# ARE CLOSER THAN THEY APPEAR

IT HAS been said that you shouldn't spend your time looking backward because "something may be gaining on you." It has often been said that in the African Serengeti, the slowest gazelle must be faster than the fastest lion or it will be eaten. The slowest lion must be faster than the fastest gazelle or it will starve. When the sun comes up, it doesn't matter whether you are a lion or gazelle, you'd better be running. As drivers speeding down the highway of life, it is important that you keep in mind the fact that there is always someone else willing to run you off the road. Just as importantly, realizing that they may be nipping at your heels and closer than you initially anticipated ought to help kick your responses into overdrive as you practice defensive driving. Even still, taking the time to look in the rearview mirror to see where you have come from—and what you left behind—before steering into your destiny is critical to success. That is, so long as you remember that the things you see behind you may be closer than you think.

As you move up the ladder of success in life, one of the things you will inevitably find are player-haters and sycophants broken down along the side of the road and hitching rides. And the one thing you can be sure that they are not interested in is changing the way things are going in their lives, your life, or anything else in the world. They are just focused on draining you dry and dropping you off so that you can sleep in the alleys with them. Former U.S. President Woodrow Wilson best summed it up when he said, "If you want to make enemies, try to change something."

When elected to serve as the spokesman for the Montgomery Improvement Association, the organization that led the famed bus boycott of the 1950s in Montgomery, Alabama, the Reverend Dr. Martin Luther King Jr. immediately recognized this fact. He acknowledged "difficult days ahead," made, in large part, by the very same culprits. The tremendous obstruction and violent fighting put up by white segregationists all through the South—and then in northern cities such as Chicago—frightened many African-Americans and alarmed the moderate white majority across the nation. But Martin sought to quell their fears and the movement's natural human tendency to resist change.[1] In some ways, leadership is a perilous business because most people resist change—and sometimes they even take their opposition to the most extreme ends. In the end, however, King never responded to the naysayers and dream slayers who carped at his heels the moment he stepped out of anonymity and onto the public stage. Instead he kept his eye on the road ahead and drove off into destiny.

I have had the privilege of knowing the Hon. Robert C. "Bobby" Scott, the United States Congressman representing the 3rd Congressional District of Virginia, a close friend and fraternity brother, for nearly 20 years. Along with fellow Congressman and mentor Alcee Hastings, he presented a framed U.S. flag that flew above the nation's Capitol to my wife and me on the occasion of our wedding day. Scott, a learned and practical politician, once told me, "It doesn't matter how loud you speak, it's what you say that counts." As an individual you were born with the gifts, talents, and capabilities to uplift and change the world—regardless of what other people have to say, or how close they may be to gaining on you.

 ## Red Light Challenge: "Overcoming Obstacles"

Oftentimes, in the hustle and bustle of everyday life, we forget to take the time to focus our efforts on the little things that mean so much: the time we get to spend with our children, the dates with our significant other, and all those little things that help to make life worth living. For many of us, the only time we do this is when we are faced with the loss of that cherished possession and the thought of never having said, "I'm sorry" or "I love you" again. Having suffered immeasurable loss through tragedies that confound the imagination, I have come to discover that taking time to "smell the roses" is important to our overall quality of life.

It was the beginning of my junior year at Hampton University in the tidewater area of Virginia when I got the message. Earlier that day I was busy scurrying around campus preparing to host a seminar with Dr. Walter Broadnax, who was then the Assistant Secretary for Health and Human Services for the Clinton administration. Later he became the president of Clark Atlanta University and he is now Distinguished Professor of Public Administration at Syracuse University. That semester I had been elected to serve as the president of the Gamma Iota chapter of Alpha Phi Alpha Fraternity, Inc., the most influential student organization at Hampton—we believed. We were sponsoring a seminar on health and wellness, which was expected to be attended by more than 500 students and faculty.

The night before, I couldn't sleep, just didn't feel right, and I had a bit of a nightmare to boot. Needless to say, I was pretty exhausted, but I had this gnawing feeling that I needed to call home. All day long, a little voice in my head repeated over and over, "Call home...call home." So what did I do? Not call home, of course. I figured, *It's a figment of my imagination. The voice will just go away if I ignore it long enough.* It didn't. About 9:30 P.M. on Sunday, September 18, 1994, after a long day of planning and organizing for the big event the next day, I put the key into the lock at my apartment door. I was met rather surprisingly by my roommate and friend, Kent Stone, who said, "Dude...your aunt called. She said you need to call home!" When I did, I learned that about five hours earlier my brother Bryant had been shot and killed while sitting in his car minding his own business.

From what I have been able to gather, Bryant, a bit of a hell-raiser but also a young man with a golden heart who meant well and loved his family and friends, got into an altercation with some fellows who wanted his car. Having spent thousands of dollars and countless hours restoring his old Chevrolet Impala, Bryant wasn't going to give it up without a fight. He bested the ring leader in a one-on-one fight. Well, it just so happens that this ringleader was a "somebody" in the gang world and decided to enact a murderous revenge that led to my brother's homicide. How true that story is, I really don't know, and on many levels it doesn't even matter.

The fact is my brother was dead and that was that. To the police department and the powers that be, he was not that relevant. Some 16 years later, they have yet to officially solve the case. Coming on the heels of my cousins McGill and James being brutally murdered in gang-style crimes that rivaled the Valentine's Day massacre standard of the early 20th century, this personal loss devastated me in ways that were shattering to the soul. I emerged from that experience many years later with my head "bloody but unbowed," and I am grateful for the opportunity it taught me to live every day as if it were my last.

Today, having been significantly and materially changed as a result of the losses that I have overcome, I want you to know that as you travel this life, you are not alone. There are people who have endured even worse than either of us and have come out better on the other side. Seek support when possible and work through the pain. Don't allow grief to overtake you and know that wherever you are, whatever you do, and however you may be feeling right now, as you face your midnight hour, God has not forgotten you!

 ### Rearview Glance: "Going Down for the Third Time"

On the 4th of July, 1992, I wanted to give up. A mantra that I closely subscribe to is one tailor made for those who have experienced tough times, *"When the going gets tough, the tough get going."* To reach your final destination with grace and gratitude, you must first begin by having the faith to believe that you are not forgotten and that you are never, ever alone. And, if you hold on just a little while longer, you cannot be denied. You see, there is something to be said about persistence and never, ever giving up.

On that fateful and festive hot summer's day, I went yachting (a first) with some friends visiting from Rhode Island. Their friends owned a beautiful boat that they tooled around in on weekends off

South Florida's intercostals waterways. As a young, 17-year-old fool, I had been swimming since I was 6, so I donned a snorkeling mask and jumped off the boat to snorkel with the fish (also a first) without fear. Having been on the school swim team at the junior high and high school levels, swimming was then, and is to this day, my favorite form of physical exercise. Little did I know, I would almost end up sleeping with the fishes—had it not been for a rope and the hand of a friend willing to pull me to safety.

As I snorkeled around in the Atlantic, just off the coast of Peanut Island in Palm Beach County, Florida, I rather enjoyed the sea life underneath me. I was seeing schools of fish and small sea animals living their lives in their own habitat. Soon I began to get tired and readied myself to go back to the yacht and lay out on the deck with everyone else. So I began swimming to the boat. And swimming...and swimming. What I didn't realize was that I was being swept out to sea, farther and farther away from the boat, in a riptide that rolled my way. I soon began to get tired. Then I began to panic. Then I began to drown. And as I began to drown, in utter disbelief no less, my life flashed before my eyes in an instant. All of my days—turned into nights—turned into days, went through my head and I reconciled myself in that instant that my moment of death had arrived.

Just then, a voice inside of me said, "Swim...swim..." and I gave it one last shot. Moments later I swam into a boat that had been anchored and there, in the middle of the ocean, was a rope. I don't know where it came from; it was just there, and I held onto it for dear life. Nothing could have been more *on time* for me in my life than that rope in the middle of the sea. After recognizing my distress, my friend, Martin Haim, who has aptly become one of Providence's finest as a decorated police officer, came out from the boat to bring me to safety and make sure that I was OK.

Today, even when you feel as if you're drowning in your own situation, I am here to remind you that your lifeline is waiting for you to grab hold of and to fight like there's no tomorrow. If you continue to hold on, just a little while longer, help is on the way! More importantly, I want you to know that when you are completely out of gas and coasting on fumes, there will be a station just around the bend. Just turn the radio off, roll down the windows, and pray! And even if you run out of gas and are coasting along the shoulder of the road, look in the rearview mirror—that just may be a tow truck behind you.

 ## Universal Road Rule: "Keep Driving Around"

One of the worst feelings in the world is to be rushing home and you're running five minutes late, only to look up and discover that you missed the last bus and are stuck along the side of the road. It's a sinking sensation that immediately puts your body into fight or flight mode, depending on the time of day, location, and neighborhood in which you have been stranded. What do you do? Well, for starters, you immediately assess the situation, consider the alternatives, and plan another means of transport—depending upon your financial resources, of course. The same is true in life when you get to the point of being overwhelmed and alone. When it seems as if the vicissitudes of life are weighing you down and you cannot move another inch, know that someone out there knows you and loves you anyway; someone knows your name.

As a child whose favorite aunt was murdered when I was 6 years old, I was dazed and confused, but I never gave up. When I lost several cousins to street violence, I wanted to throw in the towel and call it quits, but instead I hung in there—and never gave up. When two of my brothers were murdered, one after the other, on the violent streets of my hometown, I felt as if my world had come to an end. But I endured, knowing that this too shall pass. Life will knock you down from time to time but, in the oft-quoted words of Willie Jolley, "If you can look up you can get up." Regardless of how far you *think* you have fallen, never give up on your dreams.

Lastly, I want to remind you to work just a little bit harder the next time you get stuck. You may just be "three feet from gold." Author Greg Reid, a phenomenal writer and good friend, has a wonderful book he co-wrote entitled *Three Feet from Gold*, in which he interviewed individuals who had accomplished amazing things when logic says that they should have given up. How many times have you pulled off the freeway too quickly when you were searching for a location, only to discover that the place you were looking for was just a stone's throw away? As Reid would put it, you were just "three feet from gold."[2]

As the saying goes, "Success is when preparation meets opportunity." But you see, the tendency is to get complacent when we get into our comfort zone, and we tend to take our eye off the ball. My favorite book says that we should "not get tired when doing good work because, at harvest time, the bounty will be great" (see Gal. 6:9). Just keep watering the crops. Have any of you ever gotten tired—or even worse, run out of gas—at the most inopportune time? There's nothing worse than being caught unprepared and giving up as a result. Are you prepared to leap into your destiny or simmer in your own stew?

A wonderful story I heard and committed to memory years ago about two little frogs adequately sums up, I believe, what happens if you keep swimming around:

*Two frogs fell into a deep cream bowl.*
*One of which was an optimistic soul*
*But the other one took a gloomy view.*
*"I shall die," he declared, "and so will you."*
*So with a last despairing cry,*
*he kicked up his legs and said goodbye.*
*But the other frog said with a merry little grin,*
*"I can't get out, but I won't give in."*
*"I'll swim around a little bit until my strength is spent. Having done all,*
*I'll die content."*
*So slowly he swam, until it would seem,*
*his efforts began to churn the cream.*
*Then on top of the butter at last he stopped.*
*And out of the bowl he happily hopped.*
*What's the moral? It's easily found.*
*If you can't get out—keep swimming around!*

 **Real Life Road Map:
"Never Give In,
Never Give Out, Never Give Up!"**

Self-care is critically important in achieving ultimate success. It is what truly makes the difference in whether you get to your destination at all and, most importantly, whether you arrive alive. Therefore, it is important that you begin by addressing three critical areas that can stifle your progress, slow you down, require you to make serious repairs or, much worse, leave you stranded as you ease on down the road. These areas include fear, loss, and yourself.

The great American President Franklin Delano Roosevelt once said, "The only thing we have to fear is fear itself." While this is indeed correct, one of the toughest changes we can make in life is tackling our greatest fears. Here are some helpful suggestions to move you toward the ultimate goal of overcoming overwhelming obstacles.

## Take Baby Steps

No one is born sprinting marathons. Each of us, advanced as we may be in adulthood, all started out the same way: we had to crawl before we could walk. As you begin to tackle your fears and face them head on, ease into them and take "baby steps" before you go full speed ahead.

## Encourage Yourself

My mother often told me that it was a "mighty poor frog that doesn't praise his own pond." As you travel along your way, whether riding alone or with the company of passengers, sometimes you will have to pat your own self on the back if no one else will. You must see the value in *you* before anyone else will and be willing to take a chance on you.

## Push the Envelope

The only way that you are going to get anywhere in life is when you are willing to push the envelope a little bit and explore new territory. Moreover, you have to be willing to get out of your comfort zone if you are going to achieve any modicum of positive change and character development. Confront your fears and face them head on, knowing that, if you run from them again, you'll be running for the rest of your life.

## Overcome Loss

Enduring tragedy and loss is a tough thing to do. Sometimes the simple act of getting out of bed can be painful and impossible to achieve when you have had the wind taken out of your sails. Learning how to overcome that loss and use it as fuel to stoke your life's work and passion is the overarching goal when faced with insurmountable heartache.

## Deal With It

The best way to deal with loss is to do just that—deal with it. When we are faced with traumatic losses, we often do everything we can to avoid the reality of the major change we just experienced. Instead we try to ignore it. We work longer and don't allow ourselves to grieve for the loss that we have endured, forgetting that everyone would understand and would need to grieve. As a driver, you may experience an accident which can cause injury or even death. If you are prepared and buckled up for the ride, do take the time to heal before you get behind the wheel again.

## Don't Be Afraid to Ask for Help

At times when we strive to overcome loss, we are afraid of asking for help—either personal, professional, or pastoral—to assist us as we get past the trauma. We think that asking for help shows weakness. As such, we close up, clam up, and shut ourselves off from the outside world. Don't be fooled. Nothing could be further from the truth. Someone is waiting and prepared to help you through to a new season in your life. Your reaching out to them shows the depth of an inner strength that wants to move forward.

## Don't Lose Hope

New York Yankee Hall of Famer Yogi Berra often said, "The opera ain't over until the fat lady sings." As you strive to get past major difficulties in life, know that there is hope in the future, the kind that springs eternal. It pours out from time to time to remind you that with God nothing is impossible, and without Him nothing is possible.

## Overcome Yourself

Sometimes the most difficult obstacle to overcome is yourself. As individuals, we often do a pretty rotten job of lifting ourselves up and dusting ourselves off and steeling our spines for the fight that lies ahead. Instead, we operate in a self-sabotaging mode that only leads to promises broken, failed dreams, and unfulfilled expectations. By simply getting out of your own way, you can make a huge advance forward for yourself and those you love.

## Learn to Trust Yourself

Start by learning how to trust yourself and your own instincts to do the right thing when called upon to step into action. I heard a preacher say once, "Trust is being able to go to sleep when someone else is driving." Having endured my fair share of car accidents, I completely understand the analogy as real, to-the-point, and just that simple. Learn how to listen to that positive inner voice that will always recommend the best course of action, and thereby give you a direction in which to proceed.

## Forgive Yourself

Learning how to forgive ourselves is a difficult thing to do. Often we find it easier to let others off the hook, even if they have offended us egregiously, rather than to let up on ourselves. Learning how to forgive yourself for offenses you have committed and mistakes you have made will go a long way toward helping you to sleep at night, even if there are those who may not offer you their forgiveness. Stop hitting yourself upside the head for things that you cannot redo. Learn how to forgive—and start with yourself.

## Pay Attention to Your Thoughts

Dr. Norman Vincent Peale said, "Change your thoughts and you change your world."[3] If you want to get past the limitations that you have placed upon yourself, start with the renewing of your mind. Detoxify your thoughts of all the negative images and energy that has helped to contribute to your inability to reach your breakthrough. Rebuke bad thoughts and negative perceptions as soon as they arise in thought, word, or deed, and you are well on your way toward getting over yourself.

PART TWO

## Chapter 6

# STOP, LOOK, AND LISTEN

*"Stop, look and listen...before you cross the street. Use your eyes, use your ears, and then use your feet."* This schoolyard rhyme, in use for decades at American schools, was written to help children remember the steps they should take when crossing the road. Its simple truth, however quaint, is a powerful nexus between our days in the sandbox and those in which we are long in the tooth and well down the road. As children growing up, we are taught to cross the street with care to ensure that we make it to the other side. Driving is much the same way, as we must use each of our five senses to keep us safe and help us get to where we are going. Moreover, when we prepare to move out and speed down life's highway, it behooves us to be cautious when merging into traffic.

Confucius once said, "It does not matter how slow you go, as long as you do not stop." In an instant society in which we want what we want and we want it right now, one of the most important lessons to learn when getting into the driver's seat is patience. It's important to take your time and ease into the flow of things. Only after having assessed the situation and determined that it is safe to proceed, should you ever merge into oncoming traffic. Life, as we know, is in large measure the same. The best way to enter into any new situation is simple—nice and slow. Once you are on the highway, however, use your gas pedal judiciously, but use it nonetheless.

## Brake First, Gas Second

Driving, just as in life, requires a measure of distance whereby we must calculate the odds correctly—every single time—or the results could be disastrous. The first thing you are taught to do when getting behind the wheel of a car is to put your foot on the brake, even before putting the key in the ignition and your seat belt on. After you firmly depress the brake, however, you then begin the process of adjusting your seat and mirrors, putting the car into gear, and proceeding along your way. That being said, however, it's important to remember that mistakes on the road cannot be undone—so try not to make too many.

When I was 6 years old, I couldn't wait to be 25. At 35 I wanted to be 6 again, knowing what I know now. But time keeps on slipping. As it ticks away, it is important to remember that any situation you are in can change—all it takes is pressure and time. In his book, *The Purpose Driven Life*, Rick Warren reminds us:

> There are no shortcuts to maturity. It takes years for us to grow into adulthood, and it takes a full season for fruit to mature and ripen...When you try to ripen fruit quickly it loses its flavor.[1]

Taking your time to learn life's lessons, and letting its essence sink in, is important to retention and recall in the classroom, on the road, or when you need it most in life.

Take time to smell the roses. Proceed with caution. "Be cool, honey bunny."

## STOP Red Light Challenge: "Walk Down the Hill"

Two bulls were standing at the top of a hill, an old bull and a young bull, gazing down below at a group of fine cows. The young bull says to the old bull, "Let's run down there and get one of those cows." The old bull responds: "Let's walk down there and get all of them!" The moral of this story is simple: sometimes it's more advantageous to take your time with things. As a young and impetuous political rabble-rouser, I often rushed to judgment when making decisions. As an aging older man, however, I look before I leap and take my time in the process.

On one particular occasion, I made a serious lapse in judgment when I publicly criticized a city commissioner in an untactful, if not colorful, way. My actions strained the relationship between my boss and an entire city government. I was 17 years old, a political big shot on the high school level. Yet I was completely out of my league when I decided to challenge the City of West Palm Beach and its top officials, using the local newspaper to underscore policy disagreements I had with them about what was best for my own community. During those impetuous years, I worked for an honorable public servant named Maude Ford Lee, who believed in consensus building, fact-finding, and an ability to leverage those findings to change the status quo. Through Commissioner Lee, I also came to learn many important life lessons that continue to serve me well, one of which is knowing how to pick your battles wisely. For some, this skill only comes with age.

In this particular instance, I wrote a rather scathing letter to the local newspaper, *The Palm Beach Post*, in which I criticized the mayor of West Palm Beach, Nancy Graham, and the only sitting black city commissioner at the time, Mary Hooks. I disagreed with policy positions they had taken, which I believed were contrary to the best interests of my community. Not thinking that I would actually get my article published, I committed the unpardonable sin of pitting two leading African-American politicians, who were otherwise aligned in their interests, against one another. I referred to Commissioner Hooks as "steppin' and fetchin' and the mayor as Massa' Graham". I stated that Hooks' real commitment lay not with the constituents of her district but rather with the moneyed interests who were attempting to transform our once quiet little hamlet into a place unrecognizable by its original inhabitants.

Unbeknownst to me, *The Palm Beach Post* was more than happy to bolster division and controversy, so long as it sold papers. They printed verbatim my juvenile assault against City Hall. Fuming about the insinuation, Commissioner Hooks, who would later go on to become the Florida state secretary of labor before her untimely demise, responded to me with the same amount of force and vitriol that I spewed at her. Of course she used *The Palm Beach Post* to communicate her message. Upon reading her rhetorical shot across the bow, County Commissioner Lee nearly blew a gasket when she expressed her extreme displeasure with my juvenile and shortsighted actions. Eventually, I would reconcile with Commissioner Hooks prior to her death, but what was most important about this episode was the fact that I learned one immutable fact in the game of life: be careful what you put in writing, as it just may come back to haunt you. For me, I not only regretted the trouble I had caused, I also regretted the fact that I put it on paper.

Moreover, I also learned that the purpose of the newspaper was to sell more copies. The political or community-wide fallout surrounding my very public fracas was of no consequence to the *Post*. In their opinion, I should have been satisfied simply to have my name spelled correctly. The one good thing to come out of this experience, however, was the fact that it occurred when I was 17. "Oh, to be young, dumb, and stupid!"

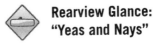

## Rearview Glance: "Yeas and Nays"

Noted American politician Adlai E. Stevenson once declared, "A hypocrite is the type of politician that would cut down a redwood tree, mount the stump, and make a speech about conservation."[2] As a young "eager beaver," I readily availed myself of campaigns large and small—striving to avoid the hypocrites, of course (when I wasn't running my own campaigns). At my young age, I usually worked for free, which would, in turn, open doors for me and provide access to the captains of power and influence. My first political campaign came when I was 16 years old. In that campaign, I helped a little known small town mayor to get elected to the Florida state house of representatives. The election, a crowded race filled with venerable community activists and notables, was a hard-fought victory that ascended the obscure small town mayor to the halls of the state capitol and beyond.

Sadly, this same individual that I worked so hard to help get elected would later go on to make a number of unfortunate decisions in her checkered political career that would mar her public legacy. What this experience taught me, however, was the importance of having competent and sound leaders elected to represent your interests. Just as importantly, I also learned the importance of choosing associations wisely. Not every job is a good job, no matter how much it pays. Be judicious in your decisions and cautious in your approach, lest you veer off in a direction you never intended to travel.

In their 1985 Grammy Award winning performance for the song, "Bring Back the Days of Yea and Nay," famed singing sensations The Winans harmonized:

> *I remember when life was so simple. People said what they meant. They were either for it or against, but it ain't like that anymore...I remember when life was so easy. Parents were alike, through them we were taught what was right. But it ain't like that anymore....*

The Hon. Maude Ford Lee was swept into office in 1991 during a special election to fill a newly created seat on Palm Beach County's board of county commissioners. A quiet and unassuming woman who spent the bulk of her professional career advocating for children and the underprivileged, she was one public servant who led with integrity and honor during her time in public office. The historic election of Maude Ford Lee was earth-shattering on many levels in my neck of the woods. For starters, an African-American had never been elected to the board of county commissioners in the county's century-long history. Second, it wasn't until a group of concerned citizens in the county's minority community stood up and said, "We want a voice that represents our community," that anything changed in Palm Beach County. Only then did the manacles of exclusion slowly begin to unravel with the legal order of a consent decree creating single member districts as the new law of the land. Before then, elections to the county commission were held on an at-large basis, which almost always excluded minority groups in any city who consistently had their votes diluted because of majority rule. By creating geographic districts with contiguous boundaries in which an individual commissioner was elected to represent that specific area—as a resident, no less—for the first time ever the courts allowed minority communities the opportunity to elect someone from their neighborhoods to represent their interests. The year was 1990. Imagine that.

Commissioner Lee's historic election marked the first time an African-American was elected to serve on the highest governing board in the largest county east of the Mississippi River. Ever mindful of the enormous set of expectations placed upon her, Commissioner Lee endeavored to do her part to undo the systemic inequities that faced people of color in her district. She championed reform of the county's contracting process. She called attention to the plight of the local school system and how it was, in essence, failing its minority students. She created the Coalition for Black Student Achievement, a group formed to give black students a fighting chance. She secured funds to develop economic opportunity and wealth creation in long overlooked neighborhoods that had been locked out of county government. And she left public service the way she came in: with her dignity, self-respect, and a solid reputation as a square-dealing politician who let her "yeas be yea and her nays nay" (see Matt. 5:37).

 ### Universal Road Rule: "It's All Small Stuff"

Earlier I quoted the motivational speaker Jim Rohn, who once said: "Time is more valuable than money. You can get more money, but you cannot get more time." As we strive to live a life of relevance and importance in the lives of those we love, we need to remember that every day is a gift (remember, that's why we call it the present.) *Not* wasting our time on things that are not important is crucial to our ability to embrace change and achieve greatness. In short, don't get uptight when you get behind the wheel. Irrational, immature behavior only leads to more irrational, immature behavior—none of which you need. Incidents of road rage and loss of life are not uncommon amongst those who overreact when behind the wheel or forget that their vehicles are loaded weapons with a hair trigger. Be sure to handle with caution.

 **Real Life Road Map:
"Relax, Relate...Release"**

A great television show in the early 1990s, "A Different World" was about a group of hardworking, conscientious, and generally well-meaning college students at historically black (albeit fictional) Hillman College in Virginia. Modeled after my own alma mater, Hampton University, Hillman was a place that attracted the elite and urbane black students, along with first-generation hopefuls striving to go up the social ladder. Whitley Gilbert, the Magnolia Queen of Richmond, Virginia, was the quintessential representative of the typical Hillman student, and she was played in fine fashion by acclaimed actress Jasmine Guy. On one of the episodes, Guy's character Gilbert dons a yoga outfit and implores herself and others to "Relax, Relate...Release." While humorous on screen, Gilbert's character showed us once again how "more truth is told inside a joke than truth is told alone."

As a practical road map on how you can work to avoid embarrassing episodes where your ego gets ahead of your brain, try this road map out for size:

## Relax

### Try Breathing Exercises

The next time you're about to scream, why not take a deep breath instead and just breathe it out? Yes, when you feel you're about to explode, a few deep, slow breaths can do wonders!

### Change Your Work Life

Altering certain factors in your work life can make your job less stressful, more rewarding, and less demanding. If you die at your desk today, they will just replace you tomorrow!

### Change Your Thought Patterns

With practice, you can alter your thinking patterns to more positive ones, develop more trust in yourself and in those around you, and eliminate "stinkin' thinkin'." Start by praising yourself and eliminating negative thoughts that enter into your thought process.

What you think is what you become.

Change your thoughts—change your world.

## Relate

### Love Your Pets

President Harry S. Truman once said, "If you want a friend in Washington, DC, get a dog." Pets have many stress management and health benefits and can help provide you with the extra calm you need to get through your day. Walking a dog can be relaxing and social, get you out into nature (or at least out of the office), and exercise you as well! According to a study by the Minnesota Stroke Institute that followed more than 4,000 cat owners over ten years, owning a cat can dramatically reduce a person's chance of dying from heart disease.[3] People who owned cats were 30 percent less likely to suffer a heart attack. Studies have also shown that owning a pet can help keep down stress levels, helping to prevent heart disease and depression. Even watching a tank full of tropical fish may lower blood pressure, at least for a while.[4] Heart attack victims who keep pets live longer.

Caring for an animal and receiving its unconditional love can put you in touch with the best parts of your own humanity.

## Start Journaling

It is well known that confession is good for the soul. Write about your feelings and let them all out. This helps you to process them and removes some of their intensity so you're less overwhelmed by strong emotions. The practice of keeping a journal has many proven benefits for one's stress level and overall health. It can also be a helpful practice in softening Type A personality characteristics, especially if done right. The following are the best ways to use your journal as an instrument of change. You can start by keeping a record of how many times you lose your temper in a day, treat people rudely, or feel overwhelmed by frustration. Becoming more aware of your tendencies and what triggers reactions in you can be a valuable step in changing your patterns.

Cartoonist Ashley Brilliant once said, "I don't have any solution, but I certainly admire the problem."[5] As you write, however, be sure to write about solutions as well. Solving your problems on paper (rather than obsessing about them in your head) can help you to feel less overwhelmed by them. You can also look back through your journal to remember old ideas on solving new problems.

## Release

### Face Your Fears

This may sound crazy, but a good way to work past Type A tendencies is to give yourself an extra dose of what frustrates you in order to show yourself that it's not so bad. Be willing to confront the thing that has had you on the run and face it head on. And having counted the cost, you will have done so having been grateful for what you had, when you had it, and where you had it.

*Count your blessings instead of your crosses;*
*Count your gains instead of your losses.*
*Count your joys instead of your woes;*
*Count your friends instead of your foes.*
*Count your smiles instead of your tears;*
*Count your courage instead of your fears.*[6]

## Chapter 7

# TOLL ROADS

ONE OF the first realities in driving that you quickly discover is the fact that you don't own the roads—the state does. Sure, you may think you own the roads and, God forbid, may drive that way, but the fact of the matter is you've got to pay like everyone else. Whether it's indirectly through tax dollars assessed from your payroll check and sent to the government on your behalf, or the occasional toll road that you must drive on to get to where you are going more quickly, you will pay. Of course, you can try to get around a toll by finding an alternative route, but somewhere along the line you will have paid the piper for the privilege of driving on his paved streets. The same rules, I am sure you have deduced by now, apply to life as well, for you can't get ahead without having first paid your dues. Been there. Done that. Doesn't work. Trust me.

As you strive to pull out of your parking space and cruise into your greatness, please do so knowing that the road to success isn't easy, and heaven knows it's not free. You have to be willing to work hard most of the time, putting in the proper sweat equity and commitment that only comes with time served, to have any measure of credibility in society. In his book *Leading With a Limp*, Dr. Dan Allender observes that becoming a leader is a process built on maturity and service, both of which only come in time.

> It should be clear by now: leadership is all about maturity. A leader's first calling is to grow, knowing that he is the one who has the furthest distance to mature. The more we walk in the path by becoming the last and the least in our organizations, the more we become like the Alpha and Omega we long to serve.[1]

To that end, it is important to remember that our commitment to maintaining our license to live must not be short lived, but nurtured and developed over time.

### "You Must Pay"

In *Star Trek: The Next Generation*, a fictional extraterrestrial race was introduced on the show known as the *Ferengi*. According to Wikipedia, "they and their culture are characterized by a mercantile obsession with profit and trade and their constant effort to swindle people into bad deals...."[2] Like most of their culture, their religion is based on capitalism: they offer prayers and monetary offerings to a "Blessed Exchequer" in hopes of entering "The Divine Treasury" upon death and fear an afterlife spent in "The Vault of Eternal Destitution." While fictional in nature, the Ferengi offered a glimpse into the human psyche in which everything is based upon some form of compensation. In their world, everything costs and their constant mantra, "You must pay!" is a consistent reminder to all of us that, on some level, nothing in this world is free. Just as importantly, assuming that you can hopscotch your way to the top of your chosen field of endeavor is foolhardy at best, and will only lead to disappointment and disillusionment in the final analysis.

In Chapter I, we learned that having a license is a privilege. To maintain said privileges, you must follow the rules of the road as prescribed by the state you are in. Moreover, part of the "rules of the road" include assessments in the form of tolls every now and again. So don't forget your wallet when you head out on the highway! What we learn from toll roads, however, is the fact that it's easier to do the right thing first, by paying your dues and not being a scofflaw, than it is to cut corners and cheat your way to your final destination. You may get away with it in the short term, but at the end of the day, you will get caught. By observing the rules of the road, however, we all start out with a foundation for success that can't be denied for not having followed the rules.

 ### Red Light Challenge: "Hurry Up and Wait"

Having been called to ministry early on in life, I learned very quickly that the talents and gifts I was granted at birth would go a long way in service to humankind. Having an ability to sing, write, speak, and communicate to the masses in a manner that spoke to the very soul of the individual was unusual, some would say. What many saw as an overflow of gifting, however, some in leadership under whom I have served have generally found those gifts to be incompatible with their own ability to influence and lead others. Even though I made a point of letting them know, through expressed and implied communications, that I was not interested in usurping their authority, I still found myself shuffled to the back and told to "hurry up and wait." To exacerbate matters, because I was relatively young, the challenge of someone at my early age with my abilities was frequently seen as a harbinger of things to come, and that, in their estimation, was something they weren't quite prepared for. Being who I am has taught me that in order for me to get to where I wanted to go in life, I had to make my own way, while continuing to work in the vineyard of leadership and service—doing so with a willing heart and a smile on my face.

When I was 22 years old, I started a special events consulting firm whose aim was to assist organizations and corporations large and small to conduct hotel site selections and contract negotiations for meetings, conferences, and events that the groups were planning. On one such occasion, I had the opportunity to bid on a contract that would have meant over $1 million in revenue for the company. I did everything I could to get that contract. I attended meetings, conducted briefings, and wined and dined the organization's leadership in hopes of an affirmative response. When the day of reckoning arrived, however, I discovered that I was not awarded the contract. When I inquired as to why, I was shocked to learn that it was simply because I was 22 years old. Nothing more, nothing less. "When you have been doing this for a longer period of time, call us back and we will talk." That's it. Nothing too complicated about that.

It was then, however, that I learned an unwritten rule in life that stays with me to this day: you have to pay your dues, and there is simply no way around it. Now, for those with a good dose of gumption and a gang of get up and go, creating your own niche where none exists may be the solution for you. For those who attempt to travel the traditional route, pop in a CD, roll down the windows, and slowly exhale. It's going to be awhile.

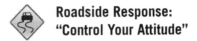

### Roadside Response: "Control Your Attitude"

When faced with a situation that has the potential to take the air out of your tires, especially if through no fault of your own, and you are buffeted with challenges from every side that would make a lesser individual weak at the knees, it is important to respond with the right attitude. Charles Swindoll once said, "We cannot control what happens to us but we can control our attitude towards what happens to us."[3] In life, you will be faced with trials and tribulations that will work to try your soul. You should always remember, however, that your response dictates just how that external situation will affect you. Will it be water off a duck's back or water inside a sinking ship? You decide.

In his uplifting CD and DVD sermon series, "The 10 Commandments for Working in a Hostile Environment," Bishop T.D. Jakes speaks to the importance of not allowing the environment you are in to get inside of you, for fear of contamination and an ultimate sinking of the ship. In the piece, Jakes uses the analogy of a ship sailing on the high seas. So long as the water stays outside of the ship, the sailors and crew are safe. Once that water penetrates the inner sanctum of the vessel, however, expect all hell to break loose.[4]

As you travel through this life, it is also important to remember to not let anything negative get inside you, whether it be negative thoughts or feelings projected onto you by others. You are what you think, therefore steer clear of hostile attitudes and thoughts about what other people believe that you should be doing, or, just as important, who you are. In short, you are good enough and smart enough to compete and win with the best of them. Just take your time and don't take it personally when you discover that there are those who are unenlightened who think that you should wait your turn. They also think that the earth is flat. Forgive them—they don't know any better. Moreover, they are not going to change anytime soon, thus your time may be better spent—not wasting it on them.

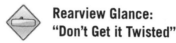

## Rearview Glance: "Don't Get it Twisted"

The great American boxing icon, Joe Louis, "The Brown Bomber," once declared, *"Everything costs a lot of money when you haven't got any."* He sure was right about that! As a poor country boy from the sticks of Florida, Louis' message particularly resonated with me as I came of age in the economic doldrums of the early 1980s. In fact, times were so tough and money so hard to come by, every time I would ask for money my Uncle James, my mother's oldest sibling, would shout, "Reaganomics!" and simply walk away. This generally meant that I wasn't going to get a dime (as he honestly didn't have one to give). What he did give me, however, was the impetus to get off my rear end and go make some money for myself, and so I looked for a part-time job on the day I turned 14.

In various cultures and countries across the globe, the concept of self-determination is one that runs strong and deep in those who are not looking for a handout in the world but a hand-up so that they can make it on their own. Having been reared in a fiercely independent family that emphasized the importance of standing on one's own two feet, my ability to fend for myself was ingrained early. By the time I entered high school, I had tired of wearing hand-me-downs and Goodwill clothes, and decided that hard work in the form of an afterschool job would be my track toward financial independence. During the late 1980s, the American economy was beginning to tighten, but with a little perseverance and a lot of shoe leather, there was work out there for me—and I was determined to find it. What these early economic lessons taught me, however, was the central importance of work.

Nothing in life is free, I was taught, and anything free isn't worth much anyway. As such, I immediately turned to my local neighborhood grocery store and the largest employer in the state of Florida, Publix Supermarkets. At Publix I found a job as a "bag boy" sacking groceries for customers at the checkout line and helping them to their cars. Although the pay was modest at the time ($2.50 an hour), it was more than enough to help me buy some of the things that I wanted. Mom supplied the food, clothing, and shelter; everything else was up to me. To that end, I rose to the occasion, spending four days a week after school and on the weekends, smiling and bagging my way to a legitimate small fortune for a kid from the wrong side of the tracks.

My time at Publix, however, was no bed of roses. It was a true introduction to the way the world really worked and just how it viewed the way I fit into the equation. One customer in particular, an elderly man, seemed to take exceptional delight in taunting me every time he came to the store. As a retiree with not much to do, it just so happens that he came in the same time each day, and he seemed to seek me out for a verbal taunting. "You know you're a gold brick, don't you?" he would say as he perused the aisles or checked out of the store during his daily rounds. "You're never going to amount to anything at the rate you're going," he would say, to my bemusement and dismay.

To make matters worse, other verbal lashings came from a co-worker who saw it as his mission to deflate my self-esteem. "Who do you think you are, Mr. Class President, with all of your fancy words? You're never going anywhere and that's not going to change." Even still, despite the daily fusillade that would accompany my time at work, I knew that a job was a means to an end, and two naysayers couldn't stop me from crossing that finish line. After all, they were simply playing the roles that the universe had subscribed to them in helping to push me faster and further than I ever believed possible. In the immortal words of Maya Angelou, "Still I Rise."

After two full school years and summers chasing shopping carts, I moved on from bag man and graduated to bigger and better things. I soon tried my luck at the new Chuck E. Cheese's restaurant that was opening up less than a mile from our apartment complex. At Chuck E. Cheese's, I learned how to deal effectively with small kids (and irrational parents) as a host for children's birthday parties. In the middle of the parties, I would magically transform myself from an ordinary pizza delivery guy to a big gray, lovable rat that danced and sang to the music. After my grand performance, I would seemingly reappear as a doting party host, and the children were none the wiser.

More importantly, however, this gig paid well! At 16 years old, I was regularly making nearly $1,000 a week slinging breadsticks and birthday cake to Palm Beach County's well-heeled kids. With that job, I was able to purchase my first automobile, buy all of my own school clothes, pay for the majority of my after-school activities, save some money, and give my mother a few bucks toward the bills. All of this made me enormously proud. This newfound largess did not come without a price, however, as my grades in school began to falter as a result of my part-time employment and extracurricular endeavors. My real passion was politics, but my Achilles heel was mathematics. I flunked my Algebra course and would have to go to summer school my senior year of high school. You see, I had gotten it "twisted," presuming that my extracurricular activities would compensate for my lack of having met the standards for graduation. Boy, was I wrong! As a result of my failure to heed the warning signs, I learned that prioritizing was important should I ever become successful at more than one thing at a time, and although I rather enjoyed the financial independence that having my own money provided me, it would be years before I realized that my true emphasis should have been on learning and developing my mind and, in doing so, my wallet would take care of itself.

 ## Universal Road Rule: "Buckle Up for the Long Haul"

It is important to remember that nothing happens overnight. Regardless of how talented you are and the resources that you have, there are some things that you will only achieve in life through hard work, a little luck, and time. Get used to it. More importantly, as you wait, try not to get tired with waiting, understanding that overnight successes are few and far between. Begin your journey with a firm understanding that "all things work together for the good of them who deserve to be rewarded" (see Rom. 8:28). All you have to do is to "bide your time until you get your hand out of the lion's jaw."

 ## Real Life Road Map: "Hustle While You Work"

Abraham Lincoln once said, "Things come to those who wait… but only the things left by those who hustle!"[5] As you strive to achieve the goals and live the dreams that you have held for a lifetime, it is important to remember that even in your waiting you must never stop working, for that is truly where the rubber meets the road.

Economists have estimated that those born in and coming of age in the 21st century will actually have a lower standard of living than their parents. Every one of us can do something that will sustain us in lean times.

What gifts do you have in you that you haven't stirred up recently? Maybe it's singing beautiful songs that you only share with the people in your shower. Maybe it's gardening, coordinating events, or selling anything, and you haven't had the need to do it in a while. Now is the time to consider alternative revenue streams as a means of sustaining yourself and your loved ones well into the future.

Chapter 8

# GREEN LIGHT, YELLOW LIGHT, RED LIGHT, STOP!

GARRET A. Morgan, the little-known inventor who created one of the first versions of the traffic light that he patented in 1923, did so with the express purpose of helping others to drive more safely and, as a result, save lives. Moreover, the traffic light's invention has helped guide billions of people safely across roadways all around the world. Because they are the governing entity that coordinates traffic patterns, paying close attention to traffic lights is important to everyone's safety. As in life, knowing when to proceed and when to stop is critical, not only to reach your destination but also to ensure your ultimate survival. Furthermore, interpreting those colors correctly at the appropriate place and time can make all the difference in the world to yourself and those around you.

Each year, millions of people speed on down the highways of life, only to blow a gasket or simply give out altogether. They never get to where they were destined to go because they failed to pay attention to service lights and other cautionary tales. You can avoid a similar fate by paying closer attention to the things that raise your blood pressure, which can drastically reduce your quality of life and the length of your days. To start with, understand the difference between the universal color system, which is designed to do more than just brighten a dark night on the streets.

## Green Means Go

Knowing when to go is just as important as knowing when to stop. Some of the most successful people in the world have become so because they "got in" at the right time. In fact, beginning any task with the end in mind means first having to get it in gear. And while it doesn't mean we have license to throw caution to the wind and let 'er rip, we are expected to get moving nonetheless—or get out of the way so that others can pass. In short, when you finally get to that fork in the road, take it!

*"To laugh is to risk appearing the fool. To weep is to risk appearing sentimental. To love someone is to risk not being loved in return...."* As with any new endeavor we face, one of the biggest challenges is being stopped just as we start. You know the routine: you begin something only to become stopped soon after. New gutters for the roof? Sure. Finish that college degree? Next semester. We take the necessary steps to do what we set out to, but then something gets in the way and the project is put off for another day. Well, what if that other day was today? What if you decided to finish what you started and picked up where you left off? Nothing beats a failure but a try. *"But to risk we must...for the greatest hazard in life is to risk nothing at all."*

 ### Red Light Challenge: "Incomplete Assignments"

All my life I have struggled with completing assignments. In school I was a bit of a know-it-all, so I often felt as if the assignments were beneath my academic ability and therefore weren't worth the time it took to complete them. In relationships, I would start out as the cat's meow only to regress into a Neanderthal who left the toothpaste uncovered and the toilet seat up. I have started major projects with significant and material importance to myself and the greater good, only to stop shortly after I got started. Sometimes I went back and picked them up again after serious time has elapsed, and sometimes I let them drop completely. Even finishing this book was an arduous task that pushed me to my limits. What I now know about myself is that this is an issue I must learn to overcome no matter the consequences or pain. To do so, however, will take hard work, sacrifice, and a willingness to confront my inner fears and challenge them head on. As an individual who has had his share of starts and stalls, there finally came a point in my life when I decided something had to change…and that something had to be me.

At the close of my college career at Hampton University, having suffered the loss of two brothers and my mother becoming critically injured at the hands of a drunk driver, my grades went into the toilet. Gone were the days of being on the Dean's List and a paragon for my fellow classmates, family, and friends. All this was replaced by feelings of failure and disappointment because a major dream had been delayed. Moreover, having been elected president of a campus organization that prided itself on academic achievement, the amount of sheer embarrassment I felt from not having lived up to the standard of excellence expected of me was great. I felt as if my world was caving in on me. I was stuck.

### Roadside Response: "Finishing What I Started"

In traffic parlance, the color green is generally translated as "Go!" or where I'm from, "Get to steppin'." Soon after leaving Hampton University a semester shy of graduating, I had to get it in gear as a talented but flawed candidate for a series of dead-end jobs that left me unfulfilled, unhappy, and—for the most part—broke for several years to follow. Realizing that I was not only undervaluing myself by not completing my degree requirements, I was also being told that on a biweekly basis—every time I cashed my paycheck. Finally, I had endured enough. With a looming college loan repayment, a bare living wage salary, and my own set of bills and problems, I decided to reenroll in school. I chose the University of Maryland University College to complete my degree requirements and move on to the next stage in my academic career. Gone were the days of shame and remorse for the dream that could have been. I had finally made the decision to stick to my guns and complete this task, come hell or high water. As a result of my ultimate willingness to stay the course, I earned my Bachelor of Science Degree in Social Science with a minor in Government and Politics and maintained the Dean's List the entire time. Not only did I graduate cum laude from an institution of higher education, I also graduated *"Thank You, Lordy"* because I stood the test.

I would continue to go further in my academic career, with starts and stops along the way, because for me learning is a lifelong process. In every one of these instances in which I stepped out on faith, I always seemed to land safely on something. Someone knows my name.

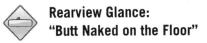

## Rearview Glance: "Butt Naked on the Floor"

It was the day that I was going back to work after three weeks of vacation to my job at the National Urban League, where I had held a variety of positions for a number of years, including special assistant to the president and chief of staff. I was in the shower getting ready for work when all of a sudden I had what I believed to be the onset of a heart attack. There I was with soap in my eyes thinking I was having the big one. As the irascible Fred Sanford in "Sanford and Son" so often declared on the 1970s hit show: "Elizabeth...I'm coming to join you, honey!" I somehow washed and dried myself off in the midst of this massive quake and made it to my bedroom where I had laid out my standard three-piece suit. *If I die in here today*, I thought, *I need to have on my suit because I am not going to let them find me in here butt naked on the floor.* After getting properly attired, I called 911 and asked for assistance. They soon dispatched two paramedics who rushed me to the hospital for immediate treatment.

Before I knew it, I was on a gurney in St. Joseph's hospital and hooked to an EKG machine that measured my heart, which was racing. Fast—very fast. They then gave me a saline solution and eventually my heart returned to normal. I was referred to a cardiologist, and after a series of tests, I discovered two very important things: first, my heart was in normal condition, and secondly, it wasn't my heart at all, it was anxiety. "Anxiety?" That's right, I ultimately came to grips with the fact that my current employment situation, while wonderful in many respects, was not what I was passionate about and called to do for the world. Just as importantly, my doctor gave me a choice: "You need to find a new job. This one is killing you." There it was, straight from the doctor's mouth. While nothing was wrong with me physically, per se, the stress from living a life of unfulfilled passion has many means of manifesting itself. For me, it was anxiety, and I had to do something about it or it would do something about me.

It was at that point in my life that I decided to walk away. In the worst U.S. economy in nearly a century, with a secure, six-figure income, I walked to the edge of a cliff, jumped off, and grew wings on my way down. "If I perish, I perish…but I am going to see the King!" (see Esther 4:16). This was a formative decision in my life, one that has made me happier as a result, as it has allowed me to take inventory of the things that are important to me and the people that I love.

As a result of my having made a very fateful (and very personal) decision to step into my greatness by doing what I was called to do, gone were the days in which I counted my chickens before they hatched, realizing that the "goose that lay the golden egg," namely my employer, paid me every other week. Now, as a small business entrepreneur I grow or cook everything that my family and I eat, and that is a sobering experience. It forces me, day by day, to trust fully in my fate and the God who keeps and sustains me, knowing that He will supply all of my needs. You see, before I chose to fully trust in God, my hope was built on nothing less than retirement funds and my assets. Today, however, that is no longer the case. I now have a better understanding of why Holy Scriptures teach us, in various forms and iterations, that God will supply our daily needs and to not worry about tomorrow. First of all, tomorrow itself is a joke for each of us as its not promised to any of us.

History records the experiences of the ancient Israelites who wandered in the wilderness for more than forty years before they stepped into their greatness. During one of those instances, God provided manna from heaven to feed His children, who would often complain about their circumstances—having actually missed a life of slavery under the Egyptians. (See Exodus 11:16-35.) In the Exodus story, God told Moses he would "rain bread from heaven" for them. He provided what he called "Manna," a new food that appeared with the morning dew and tasted as sweet as honey. The Israelites were to gather each day the amount of food they needed for that day. That day! Each day God Himself, would shower down the day's allotments and the people were simply to trust Him. For those who broke the agreement, however, they would find the food rotten the very next day. Once again, this was a reminder from God for the people to store up nothing for themselves, and to trust Him to worry about tomorrow. "Give us *this day* our *daily* bread..." Hmm...I think I've heard that somewhere!

If you are given the privilege of seeing tomorrow count yourself lucky. Live "full out" expecting that today might very well be your last. One of these days, and it won't be long, your life will flash before your eyes. Will you like what you see?

 ## Universal Road Rule: "Use What's in Your Hand"

My favorite mentor, the late Dr. William M. Batts III, often said, "If not you...then who? If not now...then when?" As I think about his legacy of activism and living life to the fullest, I have learned the importance of embracing life and all that it has to offer. One of the biggest obstacles that most people face when dealing with change is wondering just where to begin. After all, getting started is always the hardest part of any new habit we form. Whether it's exercising on a regular basis and watching what we eat, being a better parent, or going back to school, starting out slow and steady is vitally important to not burn out too quickly.

Tennis great Arthur Ashe said: "Start where you are. Use what you have. Do what you can."[1] King David is recorded in history as being known for his strength, bravery, skill as a musician, and even for his good looks. The Bible also says that David used all these strengths to build a lasting empire (see I Sam.). He used what was in his hand to get what he had. Moses is recorded as having been given the ultimate assignment of freeing his people from a murderous bondage that had lasted for over 400 years. When given this awesome task, Moses declared himself ineligible, due to his checkered past (as a murderer himself and fugitive from the law) and a stuttering tongue that no one listened to.

"What's in your hand?" God asked him.

"Nothing but a staff," Moses responded. The story goes on to say that Moses was commanded to "use what was in his hand" and toss it on the ground, where his staff became a snake (see Exod. 4).

"Now take it by the tail," he was commanded, and the snake became a staff again in the palm of Moses' hand. As you strive to live a life of freedom from guilt and of peace with yourself, the time has come for you to step into your greatness.

Now is your time. Today is your day. Take it by the tail!

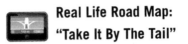 **Real Life Road Map:
"Take It By The Tail"**

- After taking stock of the talents and skills that are currently at your disposal, step into your destiny and "take it by the tail" starting today!

- Rediscover what it is that you do best and figure out a way to get paid for it.

- In today's challenging economy, people are rediscovering talents and skills that they forgot about a long time ago or never knew they had. Who knows, maybe a skill or talent you've buried in your past can propel you into your future.

- Take a personal inventory of your talents and skills by performing a self-assessment or personality profile that provides you greater clarity on who you are and what you should be doing. To find the appropriate profile that's right for you, please visit my Website at www.ArchitectOfChange.com and take a tour of our "College of Change."

- Ask yourself: "What's in my hand, and more importantly, what am I going to do with it?"

## Yellow Means Proceed With Caution

Many drivers on the highways of life incorrectly assume that a yellow light means to begin to slow down. Even worse, some believe that a yellow light means they should speed up before the light turns red. What it actually means, however, is to "proceed with caution; be judicious in your approach." The same can be said for how you progress in life. When you see cautionary tales—heed them. Nothing says "stupid" more than seeing the guy with the hockey mask and chainsaw alongside the road and stopping to ask for directions. Be smart about the way you travel through life so that you can live full and die empty.

A young boy was born, tragically, with no body, only a head that he used to communicate his wants and needs to the world. Every day, his mother used to place him on the windowsill to watch the other kids laugh and play in the streets. Every day he prayed to God, "Lord, *please* give me a body so I can play in the street like the other kids." One night Saint Peter came to the kid in a dream and told him that he was perfect just as he was and that the boy should give up any notion of getting a body. The young man persisted in prayer until one day he awoke, and lo and behold, he had an age-appropriate body for his age-appropriate self. After finding some clothes, the first thing the boy did was to run outside and play with the other kids. Suddenly, he was hit by a car careening down the street and the young boy died instantly. Moments later he was ushered into heaven where he ran into Saint Peter. "You see, kid, I told you that you should have quit while you were a head!"

On the roadways of life, take note of special omens and yellow lights that pop up every now and then. That light is blinking yellow for a reason—whether in your life, in your car, or on the street, and it would behoove you to heed it.

## Red Light Challenge: "Near Misses"

There comes a time when you are driving when you have to know how to pump the brakes. Just stop the darned thing. Hopefully, you are vigilant enough to not have to slam them hard, but if you do, brace yourself for impact because it is going to be touch and go from there on out. Not knowing to pump the brakes at the appropriate time has caused me irreparable harm on the highways and byways of life.

As a teenager, I was in my fair share of accidents and, believe it or not, I was not the person behind the wheel. I was always the unfortunate victim of negligence—either I was with someone who was not as vigilant as he should have been, or I happened to be sitting in the car when we were both the victims of someone else's negligence. Many times, this happened because someone failed to heed a yellow light. Either way, I came up short. Fortunately, I have had some "near misses" that have shaken me up a bit but otherwise left me physically unscathed. When I say "near miss," I am referring to my belief that "I nearly missed meeting my Maker and there, but for the grace of God go I...."

What these accidents did do, however, was to leave me with an inherent unease with others behind the wheel and an overprotective posture when I am behind the wheel. I'm not talking Grandma Moses— but a distant cousin. Moreover, I do not go to sleep when others drive unless there is a supreme level of comfort with the driver. Even then, I clutch the side of the door and silently pray for dear life the faster they speed down the road. I'm working on that. Until I master my fear of other people's driving, however, I will try my luck with cab service (God help me) and with tooling myself around. Yet and still, I may get there later than some, but I will get there—in one piece, I might add.

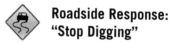

### Roadside Response: "Stop Digging"

It is often noted, "The first thing you do when you find yourself in a hole is to stop digging." Well, the same applies to how you deal with life. When warning signs pop up that caution of impending danger, if you continue on the same course and you keep on keeping on, then shame on you. The time to act is *before* you get a flat—or blow a gasket—and find yourself in need of a major overhaul or something much worse. Furthermore, failure to respond to said signs can lead to unintended consequences that sometimes we're just not ready for. Do what you can to pull over safely and immediately get things checked out before you do irreparable harm.

Sometimes in life I tend to be "stuck on stupid." I see caution signs and still attempt to speed to my destination. In every single one of those instances, however, I could have chosen to slow down or even prepare to stop. Perhaps I kept going because I already saw myself past the intersection and further down the road.

Famed New York Yankee's Coach, Yogi Berra, once said, "The future ain't what it used to be." As you realize that the time to change and adjust is *now* or you will face a radical disconnect from what really matters most, heeding the advice of those who have been down the road you are on and who are waving big orange flags is crucial. Even if you don't like the big snarly guy with the snaggletooth flashing a sign, the flag he's waving means something. Ignore these warnings at great risk of peril.

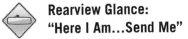

### Rearview Glance: "Here I Am...Send Me"

At age 14, I sat on the front pew of the 5th Street Church of God in West Palm Beach, Florida, and accepted the call of God on my life to preach good news to the world. Like the ancient prophet Samuel who heard the voice of God three times before he responded in the affirmative, my calling was clear and my response resolute: "Here I am, Lord. Send me" (see Isa. 6:8). From that point forward, I immersed myself in the doing of good works, hoping to make some measure of a difference in my community. At 15, I spent my Saturday afternoons at the Palm Beach County Stockade ministering to the inmates and offering them hope and encouragement. At 16, I used Sunday afternoons after church as an opportunity to reach out to the lost and the least, speaking to the homeless and to addicts under an old oak tree in the worse neighborhood of my city. Never in my wildest dreams, however, did I realize that those whom I was trying to help would, in turn, minister to me, admonishing me to avoid the broad way to destruction (see Matt. 7:13). In fact, by the time I graduated from Palm Beach Lakes Community High School in 1992, I was honored to be recognized by a local television station and Sun Bank as a "Sun Team Trust" student of the month. I was also awarded the *Palm Beach Post* "Pathfinder's Award" for community service. I received a $1,500 college scholarship for my work throughout the previous years in a ceremony fit for an Academy Award winner.

This population of the most unfortunate also taught me the importance of keeping your guard up at all times, understanding that "all shut-eye ain't sleep." Although it is important to help others, "be wise as a serpent and harmless as a dove" (see Matt. 10:16). Visiting a prison at 14, while noble, isn't necessarily the smartest thing in the world to do as a kid. Since that time, I have gone on to serve in the New York City Police Department's Auxiliary Police Program where I took a 16-week training course taught by the NYPD and walked a beat in Harlem for the 32nd Precinct. I have been certified in the art of executive protection and security on many different levels, having developed an insatiable desire early on to use my ability of discernment to read people and the caution signs they exhibit through body language, without them knowing it. Moreover, understanding how to take care of myself in various types of environments, while maintaining a sense of awareness of myself and my surroundings, has been critical to what I have become. Just as importantly, you, too, should work to hone your defensive mechanisms so that you are never "caught slipping" and can be a survivor when the "fit hits the shan"—if you know what I mean. *(We will talk about how later on in the book.)*

 ### Universal Road Rule: "Make the Right Decision"

"There's never a wrong time to make the right decision." If we all lived by that one simple creed, the world would be a demonstrably better place. Understanding how to judge effectively just how far you have gone so that you can best determine whether to proceed with caution or prepare to slow down and stop, if necessary, is an important skill to hone. When doing so, however, be sure to consider all the options available, including the red flags and yellow lights; then make the best decision for you.

There are several benefits to pausing before making a decision. First, it helps you develop a systematic approach toward solving problems. Second, and just as importantly, being deliberative in your approach gives you the opportunity to confront the issues that lay before you, while assessing the facts as they are presented—no matter how brutal they are. Then, after you have taken the right amount of time to make an informed decision, proceed from there; with a firm grasp of what your actions may mean for yourself and for others.

In his book, *Good to Great*, author Jim Collins discusses the factors that have helped to make some companies standard-bearers for their brands for generations while others went the way of the Dodo bird—that is, extinct! Part of this formula, Collins discovered, was the fact that these companies took the time to make the right decisions, heeding to the well-known mantra: "Do it right...or do it over!"

> One of the dominant themes from our research is that break-through results come about by a series of good decisions, diligently executed and accumulated on top of one another. Of course, the good-to-great companies did not have a per-fect track record. But on the whole, they made many more good decisions than bad ones....[2]

Whether confronting challenges from a business perspective or an individual one, making the right decision requires slowing down long enough to fully appreciate the consequences of each decision that we make, so that, at the very least, we do so with our eyes wide open.

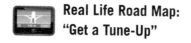 **Real Life Road Map:
"Get a Tune-Up"**

## Check Under the Hood Often

Always remember that you are your vehicle! And guess what? You only get one of *you*. If you treat your body right, it ought to give you what you need. Moreover, when you strive to live life in the fullness of joy, it is important that you check under the hood often. Look for leaks and check for odors that are unusual for your car. No one knows your vehicle better than you. If you take care of your transportation, chances are it will reciprocate, but the partnership begins with you.

## When a Light Comes On, See a Mechanic

When you get to a point where you have a nagging indicator that won't go off (i.e., headaches, nausea, or anything else out of the ordinary), the time has come for you to go in to see an expert who can diagnose the problem. Fixing a looming problem is always better than ignoring it.

## Don't Forget to Grease the Engine

Never expect to go very far without first having lubricated your engine. Whether it's your family, your friends, or your own sense of inner peace that keeps you moving forward, you have to feed what drives you with everything it needs or risk permanent damage that may not be able to be repaired.

## Red Means Stop. Really.

Whenever we encounter the color red as we travel the highways of life, we should automatically presume that this distinctive primary color indicates danger ahead. Moving forward, cutting against the grain of oncoming traffic, is done at great risk to life and limb. In driving parlance, the color red often invokes a sense of extreme caution and a deliberate slowing down of the processes that have heretofore gotten us to where we are. Whether it is a red traffic signal, red stop sign, or even a red fire engine with flashing lights, the color red should invoke for each of us, as reasonable and conscientious drivers, an ominous foreboding that something bad has the potential of happening if we ignore it. The same metaphor used to describe the dangers in red warning signs also applies to how we live our lives each and every day and our ultimate goal of achieving the longevity that each of us longs for.

Growing up in the South, I often heard the ever-present euphemism, "God takes care of fools and babies." While I can't quite figure out which one I am at various stages of my life, I do realize that He has taken care of me and has done so even though I have routinely ignored warning signs designed to keep me from driving off a cliff. As we strive to navigate this instant society of ours, we continue to live fast-paced hectic lives in which we routinely ignore what ails us and chalk it up to heartburn, indigestion, or just the way things are. We are playing with fire and are bound to get burned before it's all over. By continuing to remind ourselves, however, that "red means stop," we can put an end to the cycle of negative consequences that often prove to be life altering or long lasting because of our inattention. We can, however, extend the lease we have on life by renewing our license to live and taking our fate into our own hands before it's simply too late.

## Red Light Challenge: "Too Big for Our Britches"

According to the World Health Organization's ranking of world health systems, the issue of health and wellness around the world is something that has reached alarming rates in places like, well, the United States of America. This is an issue that must soon be addressed or we risk losing an entire generation of future leaders to the maladies created by lack of nutritional options.

> It might shock you to know that in the 2000 World Health Organization rankings of "health of population," the U.S. ranked 72nd out of the 191 countries listed. The health of the U.S. population now ranks lower than that of populations in countries like Mexico, Bosnia and Sri Lanka, and the cost associated with this growing wave of poor health now poses the biggest threat to our global society.[3]

As a poor, inner-city youth who did not have regular access to healthy options or the resources by which to exercise those options, unfortunately I had to eat what was put in front of me. Moreover, growing up in a culture that was accustomed to making something out of nothing, I consumed such items as scrapple, souse, chitterlings, and anything fried. So the potential of having butter flowing freely through my veins was far from a remote possibility.

As a junior high school student, I would often hear, "That boy is getting as wide as all outdoors," when others referred to me. In addition to growing up in an impoverished neighborhood, I had become too busy with life to see my own health warning signs. For many years I struggled with my weight until my late 20s, when I found myself in the emergency room a time or two for completely avoidable reasons. As such, my failure to exercise and eat the proper foods in my 20s caused my weight to balloon out of control and my cholesterol and high blood pressure levels to go through the roof. My health threatened to end a promising life and career before I really had an opportunity to chase after my goals and dreams. Since that time, and many diets later, I have learned the importance of maintaining optimal health standards that bring balance not only to my height-weight proportion, but also to my life as a whole. I now realize that, without my health, nothing else really matters.

As drivers speeding down the highway of life, we too can find ourselves preoccupied by the sights we see along the side of the highway and take our eye off the road. Even worse, we may fail to heed the warning signs or the "check engine" light and, in doing so, we unfortunately run the risk of damaging our vehicles to the point of inoperability. To avoid this disastrous fate, it is important to remember that no one will take care of your ride better than you. Neglecting your only means of getting around is done so at risk of injury to yourself and others. Do so at your own peril!

### Roadside Response: "Start Moving!"

As a result of a routine physical exam that revealed a plethora of preventable maladies that could easily be avoided with better nutrition and regular exercise, my doctor challenged me to take control of my health before physical ailments began to take control of me. To that end, I began a steady physical fitness regimen that allowed me to drop unwanted pounds, which not only contributed to a lower quality of life but also to potentially shortening my days because of the excess stress and strain on my body and vital organs. Just as importantly, I had to learn how to retrain both my body and my mind, as well as to alter my schedule to ensure that my newfound lifestyle could be sustained by consistency, hard work, and dedication.

As a parent who wants to see his children grow up and become individually self-sufficient, I ultimately had to change the way I lived by leading from the front and leading by example. In short, I discovered that I have to be the example I want my children to follow, particularly when it comes to healthy living, if I want them to walk in my footsteps. As such, I began by installing a personal gym that has helped me to lose the weight and keep it off. Just as importantly, I also learned that actually showing up to the gym, and then actually working out, can go a long way toward achieving my physical fitness goals. Today, having lost more than 50 pounds, I have come to live a much happier, pain-free existence. I understand that tomorrow is not promised to anyone, therefore I must start by living better today!

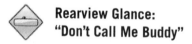

### Rearview Glance: "Don't Call Me Buddy"

One of the toughest things I have ever had to do in life was to say an early goodbye to those who meant the most to me as they "slipped the surly bonds of earth to touch the face of God." One such sad occasion came during the loss of my mentor and friend, Dr. William M. Batts III, who met an untimely demise at 57 years old. On the day before my 25th birthday in October 1999, I learned that the individual who had befriended and mentored me since I was 18 years old had died suddenly of liver cancer. He had been diagnosed and in treatment for less than two weeks before his passing. I was the only dutiful son that he ever had, and for me Batts was the closest thing to a dad that I had come to know in my fatherless existence.

William M. Batts III, an attorney by profession, served as chairman of the board of several nonprofit and philanthropic organizations during his lifetime, including the local Salvation Army and the Newport News General Hospital. These were among many institutions thirsting for the leadership and service that only "Bill" Batts could provide. I first had the privilege of meeting "Brother Batts," as I affectionately referred to him, when I served as president of my fraternity's local college chapter at Hampton University. The president of the fraternity's local alumni chapter, Batts was a no-nonsense type of guy who had served as a lieutenant colonel in the United States Army's Judge Advocate General's Corps. A diminutive man of slight stature, he towered over everyone who ever met him with a lordly rank that bespoke gentleness and collegiality. His booming voice was both unmistakable and comforting to those who needed an inspirational presence to uplift them along the way.

One particular year our area was tasked with coordinating and hosting the fraternity's state convention, which meant that Batts and I were thrust together as planning partners in what was then a working relationship. Later it would evolve into that of father and son for two willing souls who had missed the father-son relationship that each had so longed for in life. Over the course of the next seven years I would come to know and love this giant of a man who helped to shape me in ways large and small. It has been said that a mentor is "someone whose hindsight can become your foresight." As a young man who had the privilege to be mentored by an individual who counted many significant accomplishments in his own life—a distinguished career as an attorney, military officer, university administrator, and state political figure—the mentorship I received from Bill Batts was nothing short of life-changing for me. He was constantly willing to support me in my collegiate endeavors by providing advice and counsel when I needed it most, a hot meal for me when I was hungry, and a job when no one else would hire me. He gave me what I needed as I prepared to enter the world of manhood as a productive member of society. What I did not realize, however, was that this blessing of a true father-son relationship, which we both discovered later on in our lives, would be short-lived.

If there was ever a quintessential example of someone who literally worked himself into an early grave, Batts was definitely the poster child for the dreams and aspirations that could have been had he simply taken better care of his health. Sadly, he was unwilling to listen to his body when it attempted to tell him that something was horribly wrong. His problem lay in the fact that he was a severe workaholic. Often staying till all hours at the law practice he built from scratch, Batts often complained of the physical effects that his dogged schedule had on his health and quality of life. Each week when I called to check in with him, long after I left the confines of Hampton University, my "home by the sea," I would ask him how he was doing. His usual response was "Poorly, just poorly."

Not once, however, did I conceive in my wildest imagination that I would receive a call that he had passed away from a brief bout with liver cancer. In fact, it was only a few short days before his death that he even discovered he had cancer, and he had been told that he could potentially beat it with the proper mix of chemotherapy and radiation treatments. Unfortunately, however, the cancer had metastasized into an uncontrollable disease that his doctors could not treat in time. As they wheeled Batts into an examination room for one last physical before releasing him to his home for follow-up treatment, a hospital worker attempted to cheer him up. He said, "You're going to be alright, buddy...Just hold on!" With that, the sullen hero, who knew in his heart of hearts that he would not beat the disease, looked up at him and, in quintessential Bill Batts-speak, replied, "Don't call me 'buddy'!" With that, he shut his eyes and died.

Batts taught me lessons that I carry to this day about the brevity of life, placing limits on work, and knowing when to say, "Enough is enough." Through his life I learned the importance of always taking time to focus on the important things, understanding that time is of the essence, and that nothing is more important than our health!

 ### Universal Road Rule: "Don't Sit on Your Dash!"

American Idol winner Fantasia Barrino once said, "You've only got one life to live, and you're not promised a tomorrow. So, you might as well just have a good time with it."[4] A wonderful and promising young couple, Richard and Kristine Carlson, met years ago while walking along Seaver Drive at Pepperdine University in Malibu, California. They were just kids in college at the time and went on to marry and live a life together of love and mutual respect. Theirs was not, as some people might think, a typical "overnight" success story. It was many years before Richard's work struck a chord with the book *Don't Sweat the Small Stuff* and he was invited to appear on Oprah Winfrey's show. Soon after, the book became a number one bestseller all over the world.[5] But in 2006, tragedy struck and Richard Carlson died too soon at the height of his career as a best-selling author, speaker, and lecturer to groups large and small around the world.

Today, people are living sicker, dying younger, and leaving us way too soon. Just the other day I learned of the sudden death of a colleague and co-worker who seemed so full of life, vigor, and vitality. At 38 years old, his body simply gave out and he went on to be a part of the ages. As a counselor and licensed minister, I am frequently asked to speak at the funerals of loved ones and friends who have departed this life, many well before their time. At those times, I continue to remind those who are assembled that life is short, regardless of how long we live, and that we must make the most with what we have right now. If you are given the privilege of seeing tomorrow, be grateful that it is but one more opportunity to do the right thing by being the person you were called to be. Live full. Die empty!

As wayfaring strangers who shall not pass this way again, we should live each day as if it were our last and plan each day as if we will live forever. Tomorrow is not promised to anyone.

 ### Real Life Road Map: "Eliminate Type A Behaviors"

Noted writer Eric Hoffer once said, "Rudeness is the weak man's imitation of strength."[6] One of the ways in which unhealthy stress tends to manifest itself in individuals with Type A personalities, is in how they deal with others. Type A individuals typically tend to be those who are ultra competitive, have a strong orientation toward achievement, and who are so uptight that if you put a lump of coal between their cheeks, in a week you'd have a diamond. Moreover, they tend to get frustrated while waiting in line, interrupt others often, walk or talk at a rapid pace, and are always painfully aware of the time and how little of it they have to spare. Additionally, much to the chagrin of those around them, their "red flag" behavior tends to show up as impatience, rudeness, being easily upset over small things, or "having a short fuse."

Over the years, the extra stress that most Type A people experience takes a toll on their health and lifestyle. The following are some of the negative effects that are common among those exhibiting Type A tendencies and steps that can be taken to avoid such behaviors:

- Hypertension: High blood pressure is common among Type A personalities, and has been seen to be as much as 84% more of a risk among them. Ways to avoid high blood pressure include reducing levels of salt intake and increasing your exercise regimen.

- Heart Disease: Some experts predict that for those exhibiting Type A behaviors who do not take care of themselves, heart disease by age 65 is a virtual certainty. To avoid such a disastrous fate, start by developing healthy eating habits that reduce fat and unhealthy cholesterol intake, quitting smoking, and taking nutrients such as Omega 3 supplements to boost cardiovascular health.

PART
THREE

Chapter 9

# "I CAN. I WILL. I'M GOING TO!"

AMERICA'S 39<sup>TH</sup> President, Calvin Coolidge, once observed:

> Nothing in this world can take the place of persistence. Talent
> will not; nothing is more common than unsuccessful people
> with talent. Genius will not; unrewarded genius is almost a
> proverb. Education will not; the world is full of educated der-
> elicts. Persistence and determination alone are omnipotent.
> The slogan "press on" has solved and always will solve the
> problems of the human race.[1]

As an individual who learned early on in life that everything I had
and ever will have was a direct result of my having had to fight for
something, the importance of never giving up has been essential to my
overall success. I've also learned that keeping what was won through
hard fought battles requires a resolute attitude and an unwavering belief
that all things are possible for those who believe. Just as importantly,
it also requires the ability to do what I say I will do. One of the most
difficult things for most people to do is to give themselves a command
and then follow through.

I'm sure you have heard, "Watch your thoughts, they become your words. Watch your words, they become your actions. Watch your actions, they become your habits. Watch your habits, they become your character, and your character becomes your destiny." As individuals who strive to blaze new trails, it is important to realize that nothing in our lives will change for the better until we begin by changing our minds.

One of the greatest things that we can learn in life is the fact that everything begins with a thought. The Southwestern Company is a door-to-door, direct sales organization that markets children's books to families. The sales-record holder out of 150,000 salespersons in the 150-year history of Southwestern, is Theophilus Harris Davies. Davies repeated the mantra, "I Can. I Will. I'm Going To!" as he prepared to knock on 100 doors each day, 14 hours a day, six days a week, every summer for seven consecutive years. During the 7,000 hours he spent in the field, he sat in more than 5,000 homes talking to doting parents concerned about the educational advancement of their children and made more than 2,000 sales.[2] Neither rain, hail, sleet, nor snow could stop Theo's appointed rounds as he worked with diligence and aplomb. Not only did he achieve the highest records in the company's long and storied history, but he also imparted to each family he met a sense that it was possible to arrive to any destination you wanted, so long as you had the right road map to guide you. For Davies and the legions of hardworking individuals in the Southwestern sales force, a daily routine of mental maintenance and self-care helped to shape their visions for success and longevity in one of the toughest career fields known to man—door-to-door sales. For others, their story serves as a classic ~n in how a steady diet of positive affirmations and a dogged deter- to never give in, never give out, and never give up can lead to ~s and achievement. And it all starts with a simple belief.

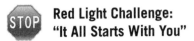

### Red Light Challenge: "It All Starts With You"

In their book, *You, Inc.*, authors Harry and Christine Clifford Beckwith remind us that, at the heart of every transaction, the first thing you ever sell is yourself.

> Inexperienced salespeople invariably start their pitches with the price and the product, then talk about the company. Only at the end, and perhaps not even then do they finally sell themselves. Experienced salespeople go in the opposite direction. They sell themselves and their organization and then discuss the product. At the end—at the very end—they say, "Now, let's talk about how little this costs, considering everything that you will get."[3]

As a company that understood this fundamental all too well, Southwestern trained its staff always to remember that the person on the other side of the door had to first trust the salesperson enough to let this complete stranger into their home. This happened long before ever getting to the point of being willing to purchase the product that the knock on the door was intended to generate in the first place.

As we prepare to get a license to live a life of freedom and abundance, understanding the core fundamentals is essential to our ultimate success. My favorite book often reminds me that to achieve any measure of success in this world, we must first believe that "God is..." and that He is a "rewarder of those who diligently seek Him" (see Heb. 11:6). Moreover, as individuals endeavoring to break out of our current situations and choose the road less traveled in pursuit of our dreams, there comes a time when all of us find ourselves becoming weary as we speed through life and run the risk of falling asleep at the wheel. To avoid this fate, sometimes it's necessary to motivate ourselves to stay awake and engaged so that we don't fall asleep and run off the road.

 ### Roadside Response: "Over, Under or Through"

As you prepare to tackle the challenges that stand defiantly in your way, taking a lesson from the Theo Davies playbook will help you go a long way toward living the life of your dreams and accomplishing your most elusive goals. Having excelled in one of the most difficult professions there is, door-to-door sales, Theo was taught each day to remember that he must "go over, under, through and around my obstacles to get to my goals."[4] This concept is the foundational thought behind the premise he was taught to repeat to himself (out loud every day). As he knocked on more than 60,000 doors during his career, he achieved either a sale at the end of the meeting, or a "no" that would spur him one step closer to a "yes." Simply put, "I Can. I Will. I'm Going To" was a state of being that defined the types of salespeople that Southwestern associates would ultimately become.

In door-to-door sales, you've got to have thick skin. You've got to be willing to be spat upon, chased with a water hose, and have the police called on you. But, if you can put up with rejection, with the resolute belief that "thars gold in dem' thar hills," then you are well on your way to sales greatness. Moreover, the overwhelming desire to succeed must be one that permeates the very fiber of your being or your days in this profession are surely numbered. In these toughest of economic challenges, you may be fighting simply to keep your car note paid. I encourage you to adopt this mantra as your own and repeat it to yourself on a regular basis, just as a weary traveler repeats things to himself and sings out loud when attempting to stay awake at the wheel.

### Rearview Glance: "Some Will. Some Won't. So What? Someone's Waiting!"

The scion of the Theo H. Davies empire, which came into fruition because of the labor and legacy left by his great-grandfather, Theo Davies, as mentioned earlier, is a trailblazing salesman who has broken some of the toughest records in the direct sales market. (He made over $50,000 in three months as a college sophomore leading the No. 1 Sales Team, and over $120,000 in eight months as a freshly minted graduate.) He did this by learning how to listen with intent, paying close attention to signs and signals, and knowing when he had outworn his welcome. The Elder Theo H. Davies, with whom he shares a historic name, emigrated to Hawaii with only two possessions to his name: his belief in God and a command of formal grammar. From there he worked his way to the executive suite of one of Hawaii's top trading companies, beginning on the bottom of the ladder before rising to the top, and ultimately becoming the chief shareholder and the architect of an extraordinary business legacy. His great grandson, a legend in his own right, also blazed a trail of corporate significance by repeating his grandfather's legacy through his chosen field of endeavor. Perhaps the greatest lesson that can be garnered from the younger Davies' success is his indomitable commitment to consistency and an ability to plan all the way to the end. He understood that to achieve any goal he set for himself, he must first start with an unflinching commitment never to take "no" as a final answer—for anything.

Author and motivational icon Napoleon Hill declared, "There are many things you cannot control, but you can control the only things that really matter: your mind and your attitude."[5] As Davies continued to beat the hot summer's pavement on the way to his next prospect and potential sale, he knew all too well that Hill's observation was not only true, but was prescient and palpable whenever he approached an unfamiliar door in hopes of making a sale. During the excruciating sales process, Davies experienced thousands of rejections that tested his attitude and state of mind—some nice, most not—as he angled for sales success. On one particular occasion, he knocked on the door of a rather agitated individual who pulled a pistol on the unassuming salesman who simply wanted to sell him some books for the children in his home. On another occasion, Davies had the police called on him when he ventured to the back of someone's home, having realized that while no one had answered the door, someone was obviously home. Unfortunately, he discovered a naked woman who screamed in horror and immediately called the authorities to report a "Peeping Tom" lurking around her property.

In spite of these difficulties, Davies believes that his toughest rejections came not from one particular person or household, but rather from the cumulative effect of the 20th or 30th "no" in a row—a situation that would make even the strongest among us ready to pack it in and call it a day. Davies, however, continued to look on the brighter side of things, reminding himself that sometimes he had to laugh at the situations he experienced to keep himself from crying. He would speak positive affirmations to himself and remind himself of the lessons he learned in Southwestern's training as he walked up to the next door. "Some will. Some won't. So what? Someone's waiting!" And then it was on to the next.

As you strive to change the way in which you have lived your life, nurtured your dreams, and stepped into your destiny, understand the fact that you will face challenges that may cause you to shrink like a wilting violet. Yet always be mindful of the power of never giving up. When faced with repeated rejection, time after time, mile after mile, door slam after door slam, Theo Davies never gave up. In doing so, he has become a shining example of the possibilities in life when we never take "no" for an answer. Even when you get dirt in your eyes, keep digging—you may be just three feet from gold.

 ## Universal Road Rule: "Talk to Yourself"

One of the concepts that the Southwestern Company stresses with its sales associates is the importance of believing in oneself and practicing "self-talk." My favorite book often reminds me that *"As a man thinketh in his heart, so is he"* (see Prov. 23:7). In short, everything in our hearts begins with our thoughts. By far the best way in which we can turn around every negative situation is with the advent of our positive thoughts. Just as importantly, the best way to attain the state of mind that enables us to overcome overwhelming obstacles is speaking positive words out loud. This helps to penetrate the soul we aim to inspire inside. To that end, understanding the fundamental premise of the mantra, "I Can. I Will. I'm Going To!" is paramount to achieving ultimate success.

"I Can" is a resolute belief that suggests, at the very minimum, "coach-ability," or the capacity to be trained. The concept of "I Can" is a challenge which suggests that, no matter how difficult the road you travel may be, "You Can" get to your desired destination by planning all the way to the end and never allowing obstacles to get in your way.

"I Will" allows the individual to arrive at the point of being able to make a decision. In short, it is the point of realizing that you can, indeed, do something about where you are, particularly with respect to where you want to go. From that point, once the decision is made, there is no turning back. In fact, the word *decide* comes from the Latin root *cidere*, which means "to cut," and is literally translated as "to cut in two" or "to cut apart," meaning to cut off your other options.[6] Once a decision is made, whether it is to get the license you need to live again or the life you desire to live for the future, coming to the point of a decision means that, in essence, there is no turning back.

"I'm Going To" is a state of mind that allows an individual to transition from making a decision to moving into action. (Five birds on a wire decide to fly off. How many are left?) Moreover, when you arrive at the point where you say to yourself, "I'm going to," it is a far cry from "I will get around to it someday." In essence, it means "I will get to it today." If not you—then who? If not now—then when? "I'm going to" implies that you have made a plan, have prepared for the long haul, and are ready for the trip to commence. When you are unconditionally committed to a goal, the attainment of that goal is already assured. I suggest you read that again and ponder its deeper meaning.

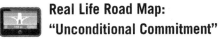

### Real Life Road Map: "Unconditional Commitment"

To begin the process of achieving the goals that we set for ourselves, we must begin with the premise that our commitment toward obtaining those goals must be unflinching and unconditional. For some, this may mean facing a number of obstacles, including headaches, heartaches, blurred vision, and extreme fatigue! Whatever this means for you, however, it all begins with a simple thought that turns into action.

### Learn to Trust Yourself

Noted Scottish author and theologian George MacDonald once said, "To be trusted is greater than being loved."[7] Just as importantly, learning to trust yourself is the equivalent of taking the first step in a miles long journey toward your final destination.

### Get a Coach or Mentor

In almost every path you take, be sure to find a mentor or counselor and learn from him or her. In fact, if you really want to be the best at what you do, get a coach or an expert to advise you, and only accept advice from the people who have what you want. Moreover, having a coach (and being a coach, for that matter) is all about asking the right questions and then finding the answers for yourself. Think of a coach as a well out of which you can pull essential information—bucket by bucket. In tapping that well, sometimes you may go every day, sometimes several times a day, and other times only when you need it.

## Forgive Yourself

The hardest thing that most people do in life is learning how to forgive themselves for mistakes that they have made and regrets that they may have. Moreover, it is important to remember that when you give yourself permission to let yourself off the hook, you unconsciously communicate to others the fact that external acceptance is not as important to you as an internal willingness to accept yourself for who you are—warts, pimples, and all!

Chapter 10

# BEWARE OF HITCHHIKERS

WHEN WE travel along the highways of life, we often must do so by ourselves. No one can run our race for us, but us—"If it is to be…it's up to me!" As we strive to get to the intersection of our hopes and our dreams, it is important to remember that sometimes it gets lonely at the top. When we get that way, we may be tempted to take on a wayward passenger simply looking for a ride from here to there. In doing so, however, always remember that the movie generally ends horribly for the well-meaning Samaritan hoping to brighten someone's day. Beware of hitchhikers.

A survey published in February 2009 in the United Kingdom found that 42 percent of all respondents to a survey about their attitudes toward hitchhiking were likely to stop and pick up a stranded traveler looking for a free ride to nowhere in particular. The survey also showed that less than 1 percent of all women nationwide would pick up a stranger, even if they had someone in the car. Men, however, were much more likely to take a drive on the wild side by stopping to engage and ultimately give an empty passenger seat to a complete stranger, about whom they really know nothing, just to ease the loneliness that the long road can invoke. In response to what it saw as an alarming statistic, the British government put safeguards in place to curtail the potential catastrophes, realizing the inherent dangers associated with what is, more often than not, a lapse in judgment.

## Every Rider Isn't Friendly

An ancient Arabian proverb states: "A fool may be known by six things: anger, without cause; speech, without profit; change, without progress; inquiry, without object; putting trust in a stranger; and mistaking foes for friends"[1] Growing up as a child, my mother often warned me, "Everyone who rides in your car and eats your food ain't your friend." This oft-repeated mantra signaled for me the importance of being wary of all persons who had not earned my trust through demonstrated action that showed they had my best interests at heart. Just as importantly, we must remember that even with our family and those who are closest to us, "All your skin-folk ain't your kinfolk." Don't get it twisted. Be that as it may, you can't be paralyzed when dealing with other people, just know your limits and be judicious when listening to someone's story. After all, everyone has an angle. What's yours?

To that end, the importance of recognizing the difference between good and bad energy early on in a relationship is a key survival instinct that each of us were born with, otherwise known as the "fight or flight syndrome." According to Esther Sternberg, author of *The Science Connecting Health and Emotions*:

> Normally, when a person is in a serene, un-stimulated state, the firing of neurons in the locus coeruleus is minimal. A novel stimulus (which could include a perception of danger or an environmental stressor such as elevated sound levels or

over-illumination), once perceived, is relayed from the sensory cortex of the brain through the hypothalamus to the brainstem. That route of signaling increases the rate of noradrenergic activity in the locus coeruleus, and the person becomes alert and attentive to the environment. Similarly, an abundance of catecholamines at neuroreceptor sites facilitates reliance on spontaneous or intuitive behaviors often related to combat or escape. If a stimulus is perceived as a threat, a more intense and prolonged discharge of the locus ceruleus activates the sympathetic division of the autonomic nervous system.

This activation is associated with specific physiological actions in the system, both directly and indirectly through the release of epinephrine (adrenaline) and to a lesser extent norepinephrine from the medulla of the adrenal glands. The release is triggered by acetylcholine released from preganglionic sympathetic nerves. The other major factor in the acute stress response is the hypothalamic-pituitary-adrenal axis.[2]

In short, each of us has an innate ability to respond to danger through the physiological response we get when we are confronted with an uncertain future. Knowing who is friend and who is foe—and responding accordingly—is a surefire way to help you get to where you are going.

 ## Red Light Challenge: "Train up a Child"

An oft-recited passage regularly echoed in my home, *"Train up a child in the way he should go: and when he is old, he will not depart from it"* (Prov. 22:6).

This meant be prepared for anything—even at an early age—and that knowledge would come back to me at the appointed place and time. As a kid growing up in the era of the kidnapping and murder of Adam Walsh, which occurred less than 50 miles from my home, no less, I was taught to be wary of strangers and to never go with anyone I didn't know—unless I did so kicking and screaming.

On July 27, 1981, Adam Walsh's mother, Revé Walsh, took him on a shopping outing to the Hollywood Mall in Hollywood, Florida, just a short drive from where I grew up. As she shopped at the Sears department store, she took her eye off her son, who soon gravitated toward a group of boys playing a video game at the store. When the group was kicked out of the store for rowdiness, Adam was mistakenly included in the roundup. He soon found himself outside and at the mercy of a heartless serial killer, identified later as Otis Toole. Within minutes, Adam was whisked away to an untimely demise. He was found beheaded in a murky grave and was recovered to be given a proper burial.

The chilling effect this crime had on parents was profound, particularly for those living in the vicinity of the crime. My mother was no less influenced by the media coverage surrounding the crime, particularly because the perpetrator was never arrested for the crime and didn't confess until decades later. As a result, my movements as a 7-year-old were severely curtailed, and from that moment on, I was taught to live with a sense of awareness and street smarts. These are skills each child should possess, particularly in today's crazy world.

## Roadside Response: "If You Can't Beat 'Em…Join 'Em"

As a result of the unfortunate experiences I have seen throughout my life, both as a child and as an adult, I have learned to develop a healthy appreciation for the role that law enforcement plays within our society. At the same time, I understand the importance of maintaining a good balance that protects the citizenry from police brutality. I have come to realize that there are a number of paradoxical lessons that have helped mold me into the individual I am today. For me, that conundrum has been at the crossroads of justice and peace.

Growing up, I could vividly recall the Liberty City riots in one of Miami's poorest neighborhoods, sparked in the wake of a notorious police brutality incident. In 1980, an unpopular—and many would say unjust—verdict was given in a 1979 case of white-on-black police brutality in which five white police officers were acquitted by an all-white jury of beating to death a black motorist after a traffic stop gone awry. According to their published reports, Miami-Dade police officers had pursued motorcyclist Arthur McDuffie in a high-speed chase that ended in the loss of McDuffie's life during a spectacular crash. What the coroner's report showed, however, was that McDuffie only sustained non-life threatening injuries and would have lived were it not for the volley of police batons, boot kicks to his upper torso, and the general barrage of blows he sustained from those who were appointed to protect and serve. After effectively ending his life right then and there, the officers allegedly placed the deceased's helmet back on his head and pretended to discover his lifeless body at the scene of the crash. Several months later, an all-white jury acquitted the officers after a brief deliberation.

Upon learning of the outcome, the city of Miami, not too far from where I grew up in poverty and desolation, exploded in a fit of anger and rage that would take decades to recover from. Having been oppressed by the boot of police brutality as a form of subjugation for years, the citizens of Liberty City were "mad as hell." (Liberty City was named after the Liberty Square Housing Projects built in the 1930s for a primarily African-American residency of poor and working class families.) They just weren't going to take it anymore and erupted in anger that boiled over into the streets. By the time the rioting ceased the morning after the verdict, over 850 people had been arrested and nearly 20 people died, including eight whites and ten blacks.

As a young man who always strived to see the three sides to every side—both sides of the argument and the truth somewhere in between—the juxtaposition of two masters has had a significant and material resonance with me for as long as I can remember. The Liberty City incident was firmly ensconced in my mind when it was followed by continued examples of an abuse of power on the part of the police. I witnessed the claims of my uncle who underwent dozens of debilitating surgeries as a result of being hog-tied and shocked with a stun gun by law enforcement officials. I also witnessed from afar the aftermath of the Rodney King verdict and the Los Angeles Riots of 1992. So I have seen very clearly how deep the divide can be between those who strive to enforce the law and those who simply want to stay out of the way of the long arm of the law.

The paradox for me, however, comes in the fact that a large part of my family's professional heritage is steeped in law enforcement. Many cousins have served as police officers, state troopers, private investigators, and the like. In fact, as a result of these two dualities being played out within my own sphere of influence, I have subsequently sought and received my own version of law enforcement training via an intensive 16-week training course as an Auxiliary Police Officer for the New York Police Department. I am also a Certified Executive Protection Professional through the American Society of Industrial Security, through which I have come to serve as the first line of defense for a veritable "who's who" of power and industry as a private security executive.

In my role as an Auxiliary Police Officer for the NYPD, I walked a beat on Lenox Avenue in Harlem, between W. 125th Street and W. 145th Street twice a week as a part of the department's 32nd Precinct. As a committed man in blue, I donned a police uniform and helped to report on criminal activity within my community. I had personally experienced negative interactions with the police as a young black boy, simply because I was who I was. At the same time I watched my relatives walk a "thin blue line" to protect and serve the members of my community. Therefore, I chose to wear the hallowed uniform of the NYPD myself, primarily because I wanted to understand—from the police officer's perspective—what it was like to be on the other end of a nightstick.

Simultaneously, however, I served as the youngest member of the executive leadership cabinet of one of the largest civil rights organizations in America, where I regularly took phone calls, read letters, and consoled grieving individuals who had been victims of state-sponsored violence at the hands of their local police departments. When I reflect upon how I was able to reconcile the two extreme realities that have come to define who I am and the fine line I have had to walk with regard to my own interaction and involvement with law enforcement, I do so with a firm understanding that—side by side—these dualities are not mutually exclusive. Both can play a role in the strengthening of a family as well as the foundation of a community.

### Rearview Glance: "Kind Eyes"

As an executive protection professional, I have had the privilege of personally providing security services for many leading individuals who have been in need, at one point or another, in personal protection for themselves and/or their loved ones. Said individuals have included Magic Johnson, Mary J. Blige, Colin Powell, and others. My capacity as the director of security operations for the National Urban League included their annual conference, which attracts more than 10,000 conferees from around the country to a week-long celebration of the annual achievements of the Urban League movement. On these occasions, I have had the opportunity to personally meet and interact with several presidents of the United States, and those striving to be president. Many of these individuals made the trek to the Urban League conference to give their pitch for why those within this African-American constituency should elect them to lead our great nation forward.

On the many occasions I had the privilege to be in the presence of former President Bill Clinton, I found him to be an extraordinarily engaging individual who, to his credit, never forgets a face that he has come in contact with. On one such occasion, for example, I was standing behind the stage at the groundbreaking ceremony for the Martin Luther King Jr. National Memorial in Washington, DC, providing security for the likes of Oprah Winfrey and Muhammad Ali as they prepared to go on stage. President Clinton approached me directly to greet me, as he always did whenever we met, and to inquire about my family and all that was going on in my life. He seemingly remembered the last conversation we had some time before. On another occasion, I had the opportunity to tour the George R. Brown Convention Center in Houston, Texas, with former President Clinton, former President George Herbert Walker Bush, and his wife, former First Lady Barbara Bush, as well as then Senator Barack Obama (the second time we had met at that point). This was less than a week after Hurricane Katrina swept through the Gulf Coast region and scattered countless displaced citizens to such far-flung places as Iowa, Indiana, and of course Houston. On this occasion, I found the former presidents, Mrs. Bush, and Barack Obama all to be amiable, kind, and sincerely interested in doing all they could to alleviate the suffering of their fellow Americans in their hour of need.

With all that, however, I can truly say that, to this day, one of the most surreal and memorable experiences I have ever had in my life came about as a result of my having made a personal connection with number 43 on the rostrum of American leaders. I met President George W. Bush for the first time in Detroit, Michigan.

During his tenure as president of the United States, George Bush was often derided for what others perceived as his naiveté when it came to dealing with people whom he did not know as well as he should have. In fact, when meeting Russian President Vladimir Putin, President Bush remarked that he looked into his eyes and could see his soul. Many people, as a result, mocked and scorned the president for having made such a claim, but there is something to be said about discerning someone else's character. During the 2004 National Urban League Conference at the Joe Louis Arena in America's "Motor City," I sat in the front row of an overflowing ballroom as President Bush pressed his case for reelection to the presidency. He was addressing a skeptical audience. Many assembled within the group were long-time registered Democrats who had not supported the president during his first campaign and weren't necessarily inclined to support him a second time around. The National Urban League itself has always maintained an atmosphere of neutrality and nonpartisanship in its efforts. The NUL had realized nearly a century earlier that it had no permanent friends or permanent enemies—only permanent interests—and therefore, it has assiduously aimed to govern itself accordingly. However, the thought of confronting a potentially hostile group of non-supporters must have been ever-present in the mind of the president as he stood at the podium and tried to convince the audience that he had their best interests at heart. And that's where I come in...

From my seat between the Reverends Jesse Jackson and Al Sharpton in the front row, I sensed that the president was potentially struggling in dangerous waters. Therefore, I endeavored to make his swim around the pond as enjoyable as possible. I sat up straight, smiled with encouragement, and listened attentively as President Bush spoke of the gains that the African-American community had made during his first term of office. During his speech, I noticed that the president of the United States of America, the leader of the free world no less, was fixated on me for the entirety of his speech. There he was, the most powerful person on the planet, locked in on me and absorbing all the positive energy I could telepathically send his way. I imagined he was looking forward to getting off the stage and back to his awaiting motorcade, which would whisk him to the familiar confines of a much friendlier audience than the one he was addressing in Detroit that afternoon. But for the next 30 minutes or so, President Bush spoke of his achievements while looking at me. He made jokes and anecdotes while looking at me. He strived to make an impact—even if it was just a slight one—all the while looking at me. This forced me, in my own head, to question my sense of sanity because surely the president of the United States couldn't be fixated on little old me.

Upon completion of his speech, however, after the tepid applause died down, the President of the United States of America headed straight for me walking at a better-than-brisk pace. Upon reaching me at the front row, President Bush put his arms around my shoulder and whispered in my ear. While I had been told this before throughout my life, it had not quite resonated with me the same way as it did when reinforced by the likes of the president. "You know, I watched you my entire speech. And I just wanted to tell you… you've got kind eyes!" Having been taken aback at the unexpected compliment, I simply thanked the president for his kind words and encouraged him to continue fighting the good fight of faith as he traveled along his way.

The unique experience I had with President Bush, as well as ones I have had with others, reemphasized an immutable fact that continues to reverberate with me to this day. It is one that I take from the scriptures of old: "You shall know a tree by the fruit it bears" (see Matt. 12:33; Luke 6:43-44). From this singular experience with the President of the United States, I discerned that he, too, was just as vulnerable and as human as everyone else, and he discerned that I was part of the "friendly forces." As such, one's ability to discern the good and bad in individuals can go a long way toward each of us achieving a longevity in life that has eluded others who simply placed their trust in the wrong individuals.

## Universal Road Rule: "Don't Mess With Strangers"

Year after year, we hear horrible stories of young children who seemingly vanish off the face of the earth, rarely to be heard from again. In fact, some of those children have resurfaced, sometimes years later, to remind us of the dangers lurking out there. Through the eyes of such victims as Elizabeth Smart and others who survived the horrors of their abductors, we can also learn important lessons to help prevent other children from becoming victims themselves. As parents and well-meaning adults, the greatest responsibility that we have is keeping our children safe. We put bars on our windows and alarms on our doors just to keep those who would mean them harm far away from their bedrooms. What we can't do, however, is watch over them 24/7, even if we are the most overzealous parents. As their guardians and protectors, we are tasked with teaching them the skills they will need to get back home to us safe and sound.

## Real Life Road Map: "Five Safety Tips That May Save Your Life"

One of the toughest jobs we have as wayfaring travelers along the highways and byways of life is to always be cognizant of the fact that everyone on the road is not as well-intentioned as ourselves. Indeed, there are some individuals who will plot to do us harm if given the opportunity. Knowing how to deal with these individuals, as well as how to prepare ourselves for the unthinkable, should we ever be faced with it, is a means by which we can ensure that we can get to our destination safely and in one piece. As the world continues to evolve and redefine itself and its values, understanding that the world we have inherited is not the one our forefathers envisioned or intended to leave behind is critical to our own survival. Moreover, with the advent of war around the globe and acts of terrorism from enemies foreign and domestic, preparing yourself for a potential crisis in times of change is one of the smartest things that you can do to help protect yourself and your loved ones. We are seeing a global economic downturn currently sweep the world, religious extremism that has no respect for innocent life, and a soaring increase in criminal activity by those who find themselves desperate and willing to do just about anything to make ends meet. Therefore, planning for the worst case scenario has become, for many of us, a way of life in the 21st century.

Practicing situational awareness means that you know at all times what's going on around you. However, being on alert is when you stand vigilant in anticipation that something could, at any time, happen to you or those around you. If you walk out of your home, for example, and notice a car sitting out front, you may not necessarily be concerned if you recognize it as belonging to your neighbor. If you do not recognize the vehicle, however, and there happens to be a strange man sitting behind the wheel with the motor running, staring at a group of school children assembled across the street, your state of awareness may then elevate. This increased alertness is known as the "fight-or-flight syndrome," our body's natural, inborn response that prepares us to "fight" or "flee" when confronted with danger. This response is hard-wired into our brains in an area known as the hypothalamus, which when stimulated trips a series of chemical releases that prepares our body for running or holding our ground. Our respiratory rate increases, blood is diverted from the digestive tracts to our muscles, our pupils dilate, our impulses get faster, and our awareness increases dramatically.

To best protect yourself and those around you when faced with a "hair-raising" scenario that has your defensive mechanisms up, here are a few things you can do:

## Tip #1: Be Aware and Alert

- Have a Plan—Always identify an escape route, no matter where you are, just in case you need one. When sitting on an aircraft, quickly identify where the emergency exits are located. If you work in an office building, be sure to familiarize yourself with the exit routes. At home, have a fire safety plan and practice it with your family.

- Don't Panic—Most people, when confronted with an emergency, simply freeze up or panic and make decisions that are detrimental to their survival. The best way to ensure that you don't become a victim is by keeping your cool and remaining calm.

- Make Safe Transitions—Each day we make a series of "transitional movements" that help us to get from one place to the other, such as driving to work, walking to the train, riding on the elevator, etc. Be mindful of your surroundings as you move throughout your day and vary your routine from time to time, so as to confuse and befuddle anyone who may be tracking your movements.

## Tip #2: Be Careful Out There

According to law enforcement agencies across the country, crimes such as robbery and burglary generally increase during tough economic times. Factually, the tougher the times and more desperate people become, the more brazen the acts of criminal behavior. Understanding the importance of maintaining a general sense of alertness and security is critical to your very survival in the 21st century.

- Walk with Confidence—Nothing screams "attack me" more than someone walking down the street with their head down. Not only does it let a potential assailant know that you are not paying attention to what is going on around you, it also sends a subliminal message that you are a pushover who won't put up much of a fight.

- Don't Tempt Fate—Wearing excessive or flashy jewelry, exposing expensive electronic devices, and carrying high-priced handbags are sure-fire ways to invite unwanted attention to yourself. When in public, consider where you will be going before donning your best finery.

## Tip #3: Stay Alive From 9 to 5

Americans watched in horror as one from amongst its most revered citizens, a member of the United States armed forces, Major Malik Nidal Hasan, entered the protected confines of Fort Hood in Texas and began to shoot, maim, and kill innocent men and women as they went about their workday. In the wake of the worst economic down-turn in several generations, the greatest security threat that individuals and corporations will face may very well come from those whom they employ. Having a plan on how you will respond should this unfortunate fate befall you while at work, is the first and most important step in surviving a workplace massacre. If you or someone you love work in a dangerous environment, know the signs of potential workplace violence before they escalate into a dangerous situation. These include:

- Brandishing weapons at work

- Open thoughts of suicide

- Extreme paranoia

- Verbal threats

## Tip #4: Have a Safe Trip

Traveling on airplanes and mass transit systems has become a way of life for millions around the globe. Doing so, however, can be a precarious predicament in light of the events of September 11th. These days, not only do we have to worry about the usual challenges of travel such as theft while waiting at the airport, now we have to be concerned about "shoe bombers" and hijackers hell bent on death and destruction. Knowing how to protect yourself is important in arriving alive, whether traveling on a Boeing 747 or the subway.

When globetrotting from pillar to post, taking prudent and necessary precautions is crucial to your traveling safe rather than sorry. Whether you are a tourist in a strange land or trolling familiar territory, such as the area around your workplace or the downtown shopping district, staying safe while out and about can go a long way in helping to prevent you from being profiled for assault or attack. Here are a few additional pointers that you can take to ensure that you have "happy trails":

- Get "Smart Luggage"—Perhaps the easiest marks that criminals key in on are individuals who are overwhelmed with luggage and bags that they can't handle. If possible, purchase rolling luggage and smaller tote bags that don't look too expensive, are easy to manage, and at the end of the day, won't cost you more. Those traveling with heavy bags are oftentimes charged higher hotel rates in foreign countries because their likelihood of schlepping those bags across town is severely curtailed by the sheer size of the luggage.

- Button Before You Bail—Taking the necessary steps to make sure that you leave your home in such a way that burglars and other intruders are not clued in to the fact that you are away is the first and most important step in making sure that you return to find everything just the way you left it. This can be easily achieved by taking a few simple steps such as:

- Request that the Postal Service hold your mail until you return. Be sure to inform your newspaper and magazine distributors also, to avoid attracting the attention of burglars

- Make sure you have a valid passport that has more than six months before it expires. Several countries may deny entry to individuals who hold passports due for renewal within the six-month expiration window.

- Leave a copy of your itinerary with friends and relatives and be sure to check in with them at regular intervals during your trip. Also, be sure to make copies of your passport, any credit cards, and other vital documents that you may be taking with you, just in case they are lost or pick-pocketed from you—and email them to yourself.

- Carry a "To-Go" Bag—Be prepared to evacuate a dangerous situation at a moment's notice. Keep a small toiletry-sized bag filled with your valuables, medications, and other essentials that you will need if you have to leave in a hurry. Sleep with those items close to you (such as underneath the mattress) so that they can be accessed quickly and, just as importantly, are difficult to find if you are the victim of a cat-burglar.

## Tip #5: Teach Children to Beware of Strangers

Each year nearly 40,000 children are kidnapped or abducted by force, and nearly one out of six victims of sexual abuse are children under 6 years old. Beginning around the age of 3, children have the capacity to understand some of the basic aspects of personal security and protecting themselves. Start by teaching them the concept of their having a right to their own personal space that no one is allowed to violate, as well as basics such as knowing their own home address, their parents' names, and a home phone number. Also, teaching children how to watch out for abductors and the tricks that they use to lure children into harm's way is just as important a skill to impart as learning how to cross the street. To that end, here are a few helpful tips that will help keep your children safe from strangers:

- Teach children to trust their instincts. If they feel they are in danger, they should yell "Help, Police!" and run in the opposite direction of the danger.

- Conduct background searches on all daycare providers, babysitters, and teachers that your child interacts with.

- Be careful when placing identifying marks on children's clothing so that predators don't use the child's name to establish a false sense of security.

- Emphasize the "buddy system." Children should be taught to never travel alone, but be with a partner or friend at all times.

- Regularly review the security policy at your child's school and inform the school of all authorized guardians.

## Chapter II

# YOU'VE ARRIVED—NOW WHAT?

AS ANCIENT Chinese philosopher Lao Tzu so famously opined, "The journey of a thousand miles begins with the first step."[1] You've been on a lifelong trip along the highways of life and side streets of disappointment to arrive where you are today. I think it's safe to say that because you've made it this far—in essence, you've arrived. Sure, you may not have pulled up to the place you've always wanted and parked in your own private spot, but by virtue of the fact that you're still in the car and have made it to the city, you don't have far to go! In short, "You may not be who you want to be...but thank God you are not what you used to be." You, my friend, have changed. Something about you is different from what you were when you began this journey so many years ago. When you started your walk into the newness of life and passed the first milestone along the way, something about you was different. And now, the time has come for you to prepare for the next phase of your journey and move forward in your life.

One of the most difficult things we can do as human beings is to actually reach our goals, or be on the verge of a breakthrough, only to become stuck and not know how to go forward. Moreover, when we do get there, we are often like the proverbial dog chasing after the mail truck. What to do if you catch it? For most of us, we are vexed with this dilemma on a daily basis. We struggle to figure out the next stage of our life's plans after we capture the golden crown. And, as we sometimes discover, the thing we have sought after for so long in hopes that it would give us peace and prosperity is nothing more than a launching pad into an even greater calling. We may not be prepared for that calling yet, but we are equipped to assume the responsibility—if only we take the most-important step of getting out of our own way and simply using what's in our hands. A prime example of this paradigm can be found in the historical legacy of one of the greatest change agents the world has ever known, an unassuming man named Moses who went kicking and screaming into his destiny.

 **Red Light Challenge: "Move On or Die Off"**

In understanding the journey that the children of Israel took to reach their ultimate destination, often referred to as "the promised land," it's important to note that the end of the beginning of Moses' quest toward greatness began on the plains of Midian, a land approximately 200 miles due east of Egypt. The Five Books of Moses, also referred to as the Torah or Pentateuch, depending upon one's religious persuasion, tell the story. The beginning of the Book of Exodus teaches us that Moses, a fugitive on the run for murder, was a former member of the Egyptian pharaoh's house who undertook a harrowing journey to escape the judgment of his familial pursuers by spiriting away to a far-off land. Prior to his departure from the land of his birth, however, the story of Moses' ultimate journey from slavery to freedom began with a famine in the land of his forefathers. It had forced his people to move or die and, in essence, helped to condemn them all to hundreds of years of involuntary servitude before they would again taste the sweet nectar of freedom and tranquility.

American statesman Benjamin Franklin once said, "Fish and house guests stink in three days." As a young man who lived in a home in which we often took in relatives and friends who found themselves down on their luck, I too can attest to the fact that there comes a point in everyone's life when he (or she) simply wears out his welcome. In the case of Moses' ancestry, history teaches us that a major famine throughout the lands of the Middle East and northern Africa, which had previously been foreshadowed by Joseph back in Genesis chapter 42 (while he was still a prisoner, no less) had finally reached a critical point where the people of God were forced to change their physical locations in order to save their physical selves. In short, as stewards of the land that they had come to call home, they had simply outstripped the land of its nutritional resources and were forced to move to a place that could sustain them and their posterity well into the future. For them, that place was Egypt in Northeast Africa. Upon their arrival, they were greeted with open arms and a genuine willingness to assist them in their time of need, ultimately lulling them into a sense of complacency and the mistaken impression that they had "arrived" at a place of comfort and convenience and could, in essence, rest upon their laurels.

After a long and arduous journey, what the children of Israel did not realize, however, was that their stay would be longer than anticipated and not as accommodating as it was made out to be. As time went on, fears of the immigrant population gripped the wider Egyptian community. Ultimately, Joseph, the former Hebrew prisoner turned governor of Egypt, passed from the scene, and the hedge of protection that had shielded the Israelites while he was in power died when he did. The new pharaoh, upon his ascendancy to leadership, was not sensitive to their emotional connection to Joseph, a man he had never known, and he soon ensnared the people of God in his own policy of immigration reform—one that put Egypt's guests on the fast-track to slavery.

Fast forward several millennia and consider these historic implications for our collective future. As a traveler along the roads of life struggling just to make it to the next rest stop, have you ever come to a point in your journey where push has come to shove and it's simply time for you to depart from your comfort zone? Perhaps you need to do something else, if for no other reason than to survive and maintain some semblance of sanity in the process. Well, that's exactly the position in which Moses' progenitors found themselves, which would ultimately lead to the purpose for his being born—to change the world.

 ## Roadside Response: "I'm Not Worthy"

Noted American journalist Ambrose Bierce once described prayer as the ability "to ask that the laws of the universe be annulled on behalf of a single petitioner confessedly unworthy."[2] As an individual who has experienced both the outhouse and the White House, having been in projects and palaces alike, I have often felt unworthy of the favor that has been bestowed upon me throughout my life by the God who keeps and sustains me. Unlike many who have had similar life experiences as my own, I am sure that they too can confess to the temptation of feeling comfortable when having "arrived" at the place where they always wanted to be, but the difference came in when they walked away from their heritage, culture, and community.

The famed protagonist in the Hebrew liberation story, Moses, a man whose name literally means "drawn from the waters," like many of us felt safe and secure in his new environs. He had transitioned from a land of oppression and desolation to a home of hope and opportunity. In short, he had "arrived" into a new beginning, having left old things behind in a quest to start his life all over again. What Moses did not bank on, however, was that even though he had completed the transition he wanted to make and was satisfied with what he had achieved, the God of his forefathers had different plans for him. He was born with a job to do: to lead his people out of their oppressive bondage in Egypt. After more than 400 years in captivity, God declared that He had seen the misery of the Israelites and heard their cries and was appointing—of all people—Moses, a fugitive on the run, to lead them. Have any of you ever prayed for God to send a miracle? Anything will do! The children of Israel found themselves in this same predicament when their "vouchers" died and a new sheriff moved to town, a strange land to begin with.

 ## Rearview Glance: "If I Knew Then...What I Know Now!"

An ancient African proverbs proclaims, "I stand on the shoulders of those who came before me to arrive at my today. I use their shoulders to test the strength of my legs as I climb into my tomorrow." As a young man who has learned how to stand in the gap where brave hearts fear to tread, I humbly proffer my own "two cents" on the saying "*I wish I knew then...*"

## "If I knew then...what I know now...

*...I would have studied the art of communication more assiduously as a youth.*" Remember what Malcolm X said, "Education is our passport to the future, for tomorrow belongs to the people who prepare for it today."[3] The powers of the written and spoken word are two of the most effective tools in achieving your goals and objectives. Learn how to write and articulate your feelings in a clear and concise manner. If you can communicate effectively in different languages and cultures, my friend, *"as my Uncle June Bug and 'dem said, "Yus'a baaad...motor scooter!"* Read as early and often as you can, including subjects outside of your discipline, to help broaden your horizons. As the old saying goes, *"The best place to hide something is in a book."* Hmmm...I wonder why that is?

## "If I knew then...what I know now...

*...I would have learned how to temper my comments and discipline my emotions at an earlier age.*" Oscar Wilde once declared, "Experience is the name every one gives to their mistakes."[4] My mother always told me that if I lived long enough, I would make mistakes...from time to time. I have learned, however, that this is the essence of that "thing" called "life." As a young boy, it was almost expected that I was going to be "young, dumb, and stupid." As an adult that behavior is not tolerated. However, understand that *your rights end where the next person's begin!* Crossing that thin line between juvenile and adult is done at great risk and peril. What's more, know with whom you're dealing at all times and take care not to offend the wrong person! "The behinds you kick today may be the ones you kiss tomorrow!" Your job—and *your life*—may very well depend on it!

"If I knew then...what I know now...

...*I would give more, love more, and think more about the bigger picture.*" As a teenager, I came to learn too soon what it is like to lose brothers, cousins, and friends to death on the streets, *without the possibility of parole*, and it's no fun being the "last man standing." Always take the time to appreciate your loved ones and tell them how you feel. Love your brothers, help your neighbors, and lift your fellow humans. "*Service is the rent you pay for your space here on earth.*"

"*If I knew then...what I know now...*"

 ### Universal Road Rule: "Use What's in Your Hand!"

Upon receiving the ultimate assurance from God that he would succeed in his efforts of liberating the children of Israel, Moses began to offer excuse after excuse for why he wasn't fit to do the job God ordained him to do. The first excuse Moses made was that he wasn't prepared, at that point in time, to step into his greatness. "I'm not ready." This is what we ourselves traditionally do when God tells us to move out on faith. The second excuse he made was simply: "I'm not worthy." This is typically the next move we make when we fail to forgive ourselves. The third and final excuse he made was similar, declaring: "I'm not qualified," which showed a lack of understanding of what his God could do. Much worse, it was a rejection of who God was, but either way he was saying, "that dog won't hunt" when compared to what he professed to believe.

After Moses failed to dissuade God with his excuses, he gave Him one final excuse, saying: "God, these folks you haven't shown Yourself to in hundreds of years just aren't going to believe this..." Finally, God asked Moses a question that seemed obvious, "What is that in your hand?" For each of us, there is power in our hands. For many there is anointing in our hands. For some there are resources in our hands. But whatever you've got that's in your hand, use what you got to get what you need...*use what's in your hand!*

David was a "man of war," meaning he was willing to cut you if he needed to. The Bible also says that David was "prudent in speech" meaning he was an articulate man, and it says he was handsome too, which meant he had it going on. If you've got something you can do that sets you apart from everybody else, use that. If you're all that and a bag of chips, use that. If you've got a face that only a mother could love *but* you can fry some chicken and cook some greens, use that too. Whatever you have, whatever you've got, use what's in your hand!

When Moses stated that he held a simple staff in his hand, he still did not understand its significant material influence. First, the symbol of the serpent is meaningful in that the serpent was the one symbol of power and authority prevalent throughout the land of Egypt. It was a symbol worn on the crown of pharaoh himself, the physical epitome of omnipotence. To Moses, however, this same serpent represented fear and danger, and his immediate response was to run away from the gift that God had placed in his hand to lead as soon as it turned into a serpent. Have you ever run away from the gifts that God has given you? Have you used what was in your hand?

## Real Life Road Map: "Take It by the Tail!"

In the original Hebrew version of the Exodus story, to "take it by the tail" actually meant to "seize" it by the tail. The Hebrew word for seize is *tapas*, which is translated as "to catch or capture," and it expresses the idea of grasping something in one's hand in order to use it. The following three "Stop Signs" are helpful hints that will allow you to use what's in your hand and take it by the tail the next time you arrive at your new level of greatness:

### Stop Sign #1

Stop talking long enough to hear what God is trying to say to you. Moses had to listen to the voice of God and then step out on faith—and not the other way around!

### Stop Sign #2

Stop trying to dominate the conversation between yourself and your God. He doesn't need your help. Be crazy enough to believe that He has the capacity to be God all by Himself.

### Stop Sign #3

Stop leaning on your own understanding if you truly aim to be free. Admit that you don't know what you don't know and be willing to stop and ask for direction. Don't waste any more time and risk running out of gas. Seeking the advice of others who have been there often helps you to avoid dead-end alleys.

# Chapter 12

# DRIVER'S ED 101:
# THE LICENSE TO LIVE EXAM

THROUGHOUT THIS book, we have offered tips and suggestions via our Universal Road Rules and Real Life Road Maps that can help you gain your own "License to Live" as you strive to change your future. The following is a test of the basic fundamentals expounded upon in this book.

I.  "Each One Reach One" is a mentorship strategy that encourages your participation in which mentorship organization?

A.  Boys and Girls Club

B.  Big Brothers Big Sisters

C.  United Way

D.  National Urban League

2. Reclaiming your birthright is defined as which of the following?

   A. Reaffirming your uniqueness in the world by first being true to yourself and the purpose to which you have been called to fulfill.

   B. Remembering that life itself is a privilege that can be revoked at anytime. Live full and die empty.

   C. Understanding that you have been fearfully and wonderfully made in the image of the Creator; you were born with certain inalienable rights, among which are the freedom to choose a different course for yourself to live the life that you deserve.

   D. All of the above

3. Which early childhood development tool has a proven track record of success for children at early ages?

   A. Your Baby Can Read®

   B. Where There's A Will There's an A®

   C. Hooked On Phonics

   D. None of the above

4.  Paying your _____ is a fundamental prerequisite for getting to where you want to go.

    A.  Taxes

    B.  Dues

    C.  Respects

    D.  Debtors

5.  The human body needs 26 essential _____ to function efficiently and effectively.

    A.  Calories

    B.  Nutrients

    C.  Vitamins

    D.  Minerals

6.  Which phrase, often used by U.S. President Ronald Reagan when dealing with his Soviet counterparts, reminds us to be cautiously optimistic when it comes to the claims and representations of others?

    A.  "Don't talk to strangers."

    B.  "Trust, but verify."

    C.  "Never eat yellow snow."

    D.  "You will know a tree by the fruit it bears."

7.  The best way to deal with loss is to do just that—deal with it. Oftentimes when we are faced with traumatic losses, we do everything we can to avoid the reality of the major change we just experienced in our lives, so instead, we try to ignore it.

    A.  True
    B.  False

8.  "It's all small stuff" means not wasting our time on things that are not important. This ability is crucial to our ability to embrace change and achieve greatness.

    A.  True
    B.  False

9.  Changing your thought patterns requires you to:

    A.  Eliminate "stinkin' thinkin'"
    B.  Praise yourself
    C.  Change negative behaviors
    D.  All of the above
    E.  None of the above

10. It is important to remember that nothing just happens overnight.

    A. True

    B. False

11. Economists have determined that those born in and coming of age in the 21st century will actually have a _____ standard of living than that of their parents.

    A. Higher

    B. Lower

    C. Same

    D. Different

12. Which ancient leader is recorded in history as being known for his strength, bravery, skill as a musician, and even for his good looks?

    A. King David

    B. Alexander the Great

    C. Pharaoh Ramses II

    D. None of the above

13. These are signs that the time has come to go see an expert who can diagnose the problem:

    A.   Stop signs

    B.   Road flares

    C.   Nagging indicators

    D.   Flashing lights

14. What is not promised to anyone?

    A.   Riches

    B.   Fame

    C.   Glory

    D.   Tomorrow

15. High blood pressure is common among Type A personalities, and has been seen to be as much as _____ more of a risk among those with Type A characteristics.

    A.   14%

    B.   34%

    C.   54%

    D.   84%

16. "I Can" in the context of the mantra, "I Can. I Will. I'm Going To!" is:

    A. A resolute belief that suggests, at the very minimum, "coachability."

    B. A challenge that suggests that, no matter how difficult the road I travel may be, "I can" get to my desired destination by planning all the way to the end.

    C. A determination to never allow obstacles employed by ourselves or others to get in our way.

    D. All of the above

    E. None of the above

17. Coaching is about asking the right questions and then finding the answers for yourself.

    A. True

    B. False

18. As parents and well-meaning adults, the greatest responsibility that we have is:

    A. Keeping our children safe.

    B. Providing for our families

    C. Fending for ourselves

    D. Paying our taxes

19. What are some of the warning signs of dangerous co-workers?

   A.   Brandishing weapons at work

   B.   Open thoughts of suicide

   C.   Extreme paranoia

   D.   Verbal threats

   E.   All of the above

   F.   None of the above

20. Admitting that you don't know what you don't know and being willing to stop and ask for directions means that you have:

   A.   Stopped talking long enough to hear what God is trying to say.

   B.   Stopped trying to dominate the conversation between yourself and God.

   C.   Stopped leaning upon your own understanding.

   D.   All of the above

   E.   None of the above

Answer Key: 1.B 2.D 3.A 4.B 5.C 6.B 7.A 8.A 9.D 10.A 11.B 12.A 13.C 14.D 15.D 16.D 17.A 18.A 19.E 20.D

# IT'S TIME TO CHANGE DIRECTIONS!

WITHOUT QUESTION, we are all being challenged with the uncertainties of change...economic change, political and policy change, industry-specific changes, and more. And, believe it or not, you're no exception!

With every change come the seeds of tremendous opportunity.

The critical question is...

How equipped are you—right now—*today*, to embrace, adapt, and respond to change?

As an individual striving to do your best in a world of constant change, managing your life has become increasingly more difficult. My Website, www.ArchitectOfChange.com, is a unique portal that allows you the opportunity to get everything you need to be encouraged to reach your dreams. From meaningful daily affirmations, life-changing quotes, and expert content aimed to uplift and inspire, our goal is to be of great value to you as you strive to step into your greatness. Go to our Website now and sign up for our courtesy online newsletter and receive an impactful gift for you and your family absolutely free! As an added bonus, I am also providing a courtesy copy of my life-changing questionnaire, "55 Questions That Will Change Your Life," a part of my *10 Ways to Embrace Change Series*, at the end of this book.

With this great opportunity in hand, coupled with your new license to live a life of satisfaction and meaning, becoming an "Architect of Change" yourself is the next logical step that you can take toward manifesting the destiny you so richly deserve. Join us now at www.ArchitectOfChange.com and take advantage of more great online features, including:

- Free resources and relevant content

- Diagnostic tools and cool merchandise

- Interesting blogs and video content

- Expert and user-generated content

- Training events and activities

- Alternative revenue streams

- An online community

- And much, much more!

As the Architect Of Change, I am committed to helping you to live the life you so richly deserve, but the choice to change is up to you. Now is your time. Today is your day. Step into your greatness!

# 55 QUESTIONS
# THAT WILL CHANGE YOUR LIFE

*"Be honest with yourself and things will never be the same."*

1. How would you describe your personality type (i.e., calm and reserved, stressed out, etc.)?

2. What are some of the issues in your life that cause you stress and/or anxiety?

3. How do you typically react to stress and anxiety?

4. How do you generally deal with the things in your life that cause you stress and anxiety?

5. List the top five things in your life for which you are grateful.

6. How can you best express your appreciation for the things for which you are grateful?

7. Describe a situation in which you overreacted.

8. How could you have handled that situation differently?

9. What are some of the things in your life that you need to let go of?

10. Are there toxic relationships in your life that you need to let go of?

11. What do you do to relax and release stress?

12. How has your personality type affected your behavior and/or health?

13. Do you have or have you ever had pets? How have they made you feel?

14. List five things that invoke fear in your life.

15. How have you dealt with those fears in the past?

16. What are some of the steps you can take to address and overcome your fears in the future?

17. What are some of the innate talents and skills you have within you?

18. How can you use those skills right *now* to make additional money for yourself and your family?

19. How can you effectively market those skills to others?

20. What will others who know you well have to say about your level of proficiency with the innate talents and skills that you have?

21. What are some of the tasks that you have failed at in the past?

22. What could you have done differently to achieve the success you were looking for?

23. Name three examples of people who have failed on their way to success. How do they inspire you?

24. How have your past failures come to define your present?

25. What action steps can you take now to turn your negative failures into a positive future?

26. What is your philosophy on giving? Why do you give to others, if you do? If you don't, why not?

27. When was the last time you volunteered your time to help others? What was your motivation for giving of your time?

28. What talents and skills do you possess that could be used in service to others? What can you do *now* to help impact the lives of those around you? *Be specific.*

29. How much of your financial treasure do you regularly donate to charitable causes? If none, why not?

30. When was the last time you practiced a random act of kindness? How did it make you feel? *Be specific.*

31. Describe an experience in your life in which you have felt completely forgotten. How did you get past those feelings?

32. Describe an experience in which you felt like giving up on a dream and *you did*. How did it make you feel? Have you ever reconsidered exploring your dreams and, if so, what happened?

33. Describe an experience in which you felt like giving up on a dream and *you did not*. What was the outcome? How did it make you feel?

34. How do you overcome challenges and adversity?

35. What aspect of your life's story can serve as an inspiration to others?

36. What negative thoughts do you continue to hold on to that stand in the way of you truly freeing your mind?

37. How have your negative thoughts manifested themselves into negative behavior?

38. The gateways to the mind start with our eyes and ears. What do you spend your time watching, reading, and speaking about? What, if anything, does it say about the state of your mind?

39. What is the biggest battle in your mind with yourself? What steps can you take to finally emerge victorious?

40. Identify three significant mistakes you have made in the past and how you learned from them. Knowing what you know now, what would you do differently?

41. Describe your circle of friends. What role do you play in your group? Are you the smartest person in your group? If so, why—or why not?

42. What types of groups are you a member of? What purpose do they play in helping you to realize your dreams?

43. Is your membership in this group felt? Are you casually committed? Personally involved? What would others say?

44. What groups are you a member of that have not recently impacted your life in a meaningful and demonstrative way? Have you ever reevaluated your membership? If not, why not?

45. Develop a list of three organizations or groups that you would like to join and why you would like to join them that will positively impact your life. What action steps can you take right *now* to join those groups?

46. Name three things that you can do better than anyone else that you know. What do you do to continuously sharpen your skills?

47. How well do you take criticism? Is criticism something that you welcome or discourage?

48. Would others call you an expert at something? If so, what is it?

49. How do you stay motivated? What steps can you take right *now* to continue on the path toward success?

50. List five things in your life that could be improved upon. What steps can you take to begin the process of continuous improvement?

51. Identify three excuses that you have made in the past that have stood in the way of you achieving your dreams.

52. How have your own excuses become a stumbling block for future success?

53. What three steps can you take right *now* to achieve those achievable goals that you have previously abandoned?

54. Identify ten personal characteristics that have contributed to your overall success this far in life.

55. If you could change one thing right now to achieve your goals tomorrow using simply what was in your power, what would it be and why?

# ENDNOTES

## Foreword

1. Thomas Shepherd, "Must Jesus Bear the Cross Alone?," c. 1693.

## Introduction

1. Charles Dickens, *A Tale of Two Cities* (New York: Pocket Books), 2004.

2. Steven Ivory and others, eds., "State of Black America 2007: Portrait of the Black Male," *Universal Fatherhood: Black Men Sharing the Load* (New York: National Urban League, 2007), 138.

3. Malcolm Gladwell, *Outliers: The Story of Success* (New York: Little, Brown and Company, 2008), 19.

4. Callie Marie Rennison, U.S. Department of Justice, NCJ 197838, Bureau of Justice Statistics Crime Data Brief: Intimate Partner Violence, 1993-2001, at 1 (2003); http://www.ojp. usdoj.gov/bjs/pub/pdf/ipv01.pdf.

5. Joe Brogan, "Slain Riviera Teen Shot Three Times Since November; Violence Haunted Student, 18" *The Palm Beach Post,*

August 23, 1990, IB.

6. Stephanie Jones, Marc Morial, eds,. *State of Black America 2007: Portrait of the Black Male* (New York: National Urban League, 2007), 142-143.

7. William Cooper Jr., "A Black Man Dies: Why Is It Only His Mother Cries?" *The Palm Beach Post*, September 22, 1994, IB.

8. William Ernest Henley, *A Book of Verses*, 1888.

9. T.D. Jakes, *Reposition Yourself* (New York: Altria Books, 2007), 59.

10. Jenny Staletovich, "Rising Rap Chronicler of Violence Gunned Down," *The Palm Beach Post*, December 21, 1995, IB.

11. Gloria Yamato, ed., "Something About the Subject Makes it Hard to Name" *State of Black America 2007* (New York: National Urban League, 2007), 64-65.

12. http://thinkexist.com.

13. Jakes, *Reposition Yourself*, 58.

## Chapter 1

1. Mercedes Carnethon and others, eds., "State of Black America," *Black Male Life Expectancy in the United States: A Multi-level Exploration of Causes* (New York: National Urban League, 2007), 138.

2. L.E. Davis and L.D. Scott, "Young, Black and Male in Foster Care. Relationship of Negative Social Contextual Experiences to Factors Relevant to Mental Health Service Delivery," *Journal of Adolescence* 29 (2006), 721-736.

3. Arnold Rampesad and David Roessel, *The Collected Poems of Langston Hughes* (2002), 620.

4. New York State Department of Motor Vehicles (October 28, 2009); http://www.nysdmv.com/index.htm.

5. Gilbert Law Summaries. *Pocket Size Law Dictionary* (Orlando, FL:

Harcout and Company, 1997), 294-295.

6. Ibid.

7. http://www.un.org/Overview/rights.html.

8. To view the article and download a copy, visit http://www.
   architectofchange.com/blog/services/author.

9. Jill Stephney, "Black Fatherhood in the Age of Obama," *The
   Newark Ledger Star*, February 11, 2009, 1B.

10. E.J. Dionne Jr. and John J. Diulio, eds., *What's God Got to Do
    With the American Experiment?* (Washington, D.C.: The Brookings
    Institution, 2000), 123.

11. Big Brothers Big Sisters of America; Our Impact. Retrieved
    October 30, 2009, from

http://www.bbbs.org/site/c.diJKKYPLJvH/b.1632631/k.3195/
Our_Impact.htm.

## Chapter 2

1. Walter Williams, *Capitalism Magazine*, "The Cult of Anti-
   Intellectualism Amongst Blacks." Retrieved October 31, 2009,
   from http://www.capmag.com/article.asp?ID=779.

2. Ibid.

3. http://www.quotationspage.com/quote/27715.html.

4. Hillary Rodham Clinton, *It Takes a Village to Raise a Child* (New
   York: Touchstone, 1996).

5. http://thinkexist.com.

6. Double Discovery Center. History of DDC. Retrieved
   November 1, 2009, from

http://www.columbia.edu/cu/college/ddc/history.html.

## Chapter 3

1. Charles Harris Wesley, *The History of Alpha Phi Alpha: A Development in College* Life (Washington, D.C.: Foundation Publishers, 11th. Ed., 1969), 3.

2. http://www.washingtonpost.com;wpsrv/polls/sports/skins_dallas112.htm.

3. John C. Maxwell, *The 21 Irrefutable Laws of Leadership: Follow Them and People Will Follow You* (Nashville, TN: Thomas Nelson Publishers, 1998), 112.

4. Ella Wheeler Wilcox, *Custer and Other Poems* (Chicago: W.B. Conkey Company, 1896).

5. Charles Harris Wesley, *The History of Alpha Phi Alpha, a Development in College Life* (Washington, DC: Foundation Publishers, 1950).

6. Clayborne Carson, Peter Holloran, Ralph Luker, Penny A. Russell, *The Papers of Martin Luther King, Jr. Volumes 2-3* (Berkeley and Los Angeles, CA: University of California Press, 1997), 457.

7. Malcolm Gladwell, *Outliers: The Story of Success* (New York: Little, Brown and Company, 2009), 67.

8. Ibid.

9. Robert Frost. *Mountain Interval* (New York: Henry Holt and Company), 1920.

10. http://thinkexist.com.

11. http://thinkexist.com.

12. http://thinkexist.com.

13. http://thinkexist.com.

14. http://thinkexist.com.

15. Charles Dickens, *Tale of Two Cities* (New York: Pocket Books), 2004.

16. http://thinkexist.com.

17. http://thinkexist.com.

18. Jason Lazarou, MSc; Bruce H. Pomeranz, MD, PhD; Paul N. Corey, PhD, "**Incidence of Adverse Drug Reactions in Hospitalized Patients: A Meta-analysis of Prospective Studies**" *Journal of the American Medical Association*, 1998; 279:1200-1205.

## Chapter 4

1. http://thinkexist.com.

2. Basic Carpentry. Carpentry Lesson. Retrieved March 29, 2010, from http://www.carpentrypages.com/carpentrylesson.html.

3. http://thinkexist.com.

4. Marilee C. Goldberg. *The Manchester Review.* Retrieved March 30, 2010, from http://www.coachfederation.org/includes/docs/0 03AskingtheRightQuestionsasaCoachGoldbergManchest.pdf.

5. Harry C. Meserve. *Journal of Religion and Health.* Retrieved March 30, 2010, from http://www.springerlink.com/content/h32117353487g724/.

## Chapter 5

1. Donald T. Phillips, *Martin Luther King, Jr.: Inspiration & Wisdom for Challenging Times* (New York: Warner Books, 1999), 260-261.

2. Greg Reid and Sharon Lecther, *Three Feet From Gold* (New York: Sterling Publishing, 2009).

3. http://thinkexist.com.

## Chapter 6

1. Rick Warren, *The Purpose Driven Life: What On Earth Am I Here For?* (Grand Rapids, MI: Zondervan, 2002), 217.

2. http://thinkexist.com.

3. Charlene Laino, "Owning a Cat Good for the Heart?," http://www.webmd.com/heart-disease/ news/20080221/owning-a-cat-good-for-the-heart; accessed March 20, 2008.

4. APPMA, "Industry Statistics & Trends" American Pet Products Manufacturers Association, Inc, March 20, 2008.

5. http://thinkexist.com.

6. http://thinkexist.com.

## Chapter 7

1. Dan B. Allender, *Leading With a Limp: Take Full Advantage of Your Most Powerful Weakness* (Colorado Springs, CO: Waterbrook Press, 1996), 185.

2. http://en.wikipedia.org/wiki/Ferengi.

3. http://thinkexist.com/quotes/Charles_R._Swindoll/.

4. Bishop T.D. Jakes, *The 10 Commandments of Working in a Hostile Environment* (New York: Penguin Books, 2005).

5. http://thinkexist.com.

## Chapter 8

1. http://thinkexist.com.

2. Jim Collins, *Good to Great: Why Some Companies Make the Leap...And Others Don't* (New York: HarperCollins Publishers, 2001), 69.

3. World Health Organization: Health Performance Rank By

Country. Retrieved October 26, 2010 from http://www.photius.com/rankings/world_health_performance_ranks.html.

4.  http://thinkexist.com.

5.  Richard Carlson, *Don't Sweat the Small Things*, (New York: Hyperion Books, 2007).

6.  http://thinkexist.com.

## Chapter 9

1.  http://thinkexist.com.

2.  Theo H. Davies, personal interview, April 30, 2010.

3.  Harry Beckwith and Christine Cooper Beckwith, *You, Inc.: The Art of Selling Yourself* (New York: Warner Business Books, 2007), 5.

4.  Theo H. Davies, personal interview, April 30, 2010.

5.  http://thinkexist.com.

6.  Retrieved April 30, 2010 from http://www.archives.nd.edu/cgi-bin/lookup.pl?stem=de&ending=cidere

7.  http://thinkexist.com.

## Chapter 10

1.  http://thinkexist.com.

2.  Esther M. Sternberg, *Balance Within: The Science Connecting Health and Emotions* (W.H. Freeman & Company), 2003.

## Chapter 11

1.  http://thinkexist.com.

2.  http://thinkexist.com.

3. http://thinkexist.com.
4. http://thinkexist.com.

# ABOUT ELVIN DOWLING

The Architect of Change™

Office phone/fax: 877-299-1906
Website: www.ArchitectOfChange.com

Please keep in contact with me online at the following:

**Facebook:**

http://www.facebook.com/pages/
Elvin-J-Dowling/315571455592?ref=sgm

**Twitter:**

http://twitter.com/elvinjdowling

**YouTube:**

http://www.youtube.com/user/TheArchitectOfChange

**Linked In:**

http://www.linkedin.com/in/thearchitectofchange

**1:** Elvin (2nd from left) receiving the coveted "Top 40 Under Forty" Award from The Network Journal Magazine for having "Mastered the Art of Excellence."

**2:** Elvin's mother, Essie L. Dowling, pictured here on the occasion of his wedding.

**3:** Elvin and his mother after Elvin delivered a riveting keynote address.

**4:** Elvin (right) with one of his now deceased brothers, Bryant (left) at age 7 years old.

**5:** Elvin (center) with two of the world's best-selling speakers and authors, Mark Victor Hansen (left) and Les Brown (right).

**6:** Elvin, with US President Barack Obama, at the National Urban League Convention. During his tenure as NUL's Chief of Staff, Elvin has met with countless political figures, including three other US Presidents (George H.W. Bush, Bill Clinton, and George W. Bush).

**7:** Elvin (left) pictured with famed television personality, Judge Joe Brown.

**8:** Elvin (left) listening to "brotherly advice" from mentor Otto Williams, after an Alpha Phi Alpha Fraternity event of which they are both members.

# IN THE RIGHT HANDS, THIS BOOK WILL CHANGE LIVES!

Most of the people who need this message will not be looking for this book. To change their lives, you need to put a copy of this book in their hands.

> *But others (seeds) fell into good ground, and brought forth fruit, some a hundred-fold, some sixty-fold, some thirty-fold* (Matthew 13:8).

Our ministry is constantly seeking methods to find the good ground, the people who need this anointed message to change their lives. Will you help us reach these people?

> *Remember this—a farmer who plants only a few seeds will get a small crop. But the one who plants generously will get a generous crop* (2 Corinthians 9:6).

## EXTEND THIS MINISTRY BY SOWING
### 3 BOOKS, 5 BOOKS, 10 BOOKS, **OR MORE TODAY,**
#### AND BECOME A LIFE CHANGER!

Thank you,

Don Nori Sr., Publisher
Destiny Image
Since 1982